Persuasion – How to Persuade Anyone

A Practical Guide to Master the Science of Persuasion and Influence Human Behavior

Declan Evans

Table of Contents

Introduction

Do you know that persuasion occurs quicker than influence? You will usually come up with a strategy, where influence might end up happening without even trying. In order to be good at persuasion, you have to practice. Sometimes you only have one shot, so you have to make sure that you are not going to ruin your chances.

Influence can make it easier to convince someone of something. If you persuade someone and get caught and labeled as a manipulator, it can ruin your credibility. Not all forms of persuasion are bad, but some people are wary that you might be trying to control them, so if done in the wrong way, it can make them turn away from you.

Even a thirty-second ad can be persuasive. There is no time limit that says how quickly or how slowly you can persuade someone. You might have a year to persuade someone to move to a different neighborhood, or you might only have a minute to persuade them to sign a lease for a new apartment.

In either scenario, the right persuader will have no problem trying to convince the other person. If something takes too long, however, it might turn into a form of influence, or you might just have to find a different way to be persuasive.

Sometimes you do not even have to say anything; just a look can be enough to persuade. Someone might be trying on a certain outfit, and without saying it makes them look bad, the look on your face can be enough to make them realize they should choose something different.

Even though it can be short term, moments of persuasion can have long-term effects. If you did persuade someone to sign a lease within a short period of time, that lease could be for twelve months. Now that person is now committed to a certain apartment. Before you attempt to persuade, you have to ensure that it is going to be mutually beneficial for both parties.

You do not have to have a close relationship with the person you are persuading. Sometimes we can persuade a sales clerk to give us a discount or persuade a customer to go through with a larger sale. While influence requires a longer-term relationship, persuasion can be accomplished from the moment you meet someone.

You must be a persuasive person to carry through the motivation for a choice one way or another. If you come off as untrustworthy, or someone who is not authentic, it is going to be harder to be persuasive. Persuasiveness comes naturally for some, but it can certainly be learned by even the most suspicious-looking people.

Influence affects those who might have been admiring the influencer for a while, so it is easier to become influenced by them. Persuasion requires a little more work. You do not have that trust to fall back on, so you have to make sure you are building an authentic case for yourself.

Chapter 1:
What is Persuasion?

P ersuasion is something we experience on a daily basis. We are persuaded by friends and family to help out upon occasion. How does one get people to think and behave in a different manner and to follow their path? When it comes to persuasion, Robert Cialdini is well respected for some of his ideas on persuasion and how to do it successfully, whether your intentions are good or not.

According to Cialdini, there are six principles that can be used to help out with the ideas of persuasion:

- Reciprocity: where you will do a small favor for someone, and then right away ask them to do one back.
- Commitment and consistency: holds the target of doing something because they have done it in the past.
- Social proof: when you convince the target to do something because it is popular and everyone is doing it.
- Authority: your target is more likely to do something if they believe you are an authority on that topic.
- Likeability: if you can become likable and they see you as a friend, they are more likely to do what you ask.
- Scarcity: the fear that an item is going to be in short supply, so they want to get it.

Understanding Persuasion and its Significance

The main aim of every negotiation is to come to an agreement. In coming to that agreement, a major skill you need is persuasion.

Being good at persuasion is a vital part of successful negotiation. It is a very important skill for anyone who intends to have fruitful negotiations or to wield some influence over others. Persuasion is effectively marketing and selling your point of view. You have to persuade the other party to understand your viewpoint and even to accept it.

As an entrepreneur or individual going into a negotiation, you should be able to convince others to accept your ideas or your stance. Persuasion is mostly giving people reasons why they should do something in a way that would convince them to do it.

Contrary to what people believe about persuasion as a talent, it is a skill that can be learned and honed through practice.

Reasons to persuade:

- **Changing mindsets:** This appears to be the most apparent benefit of persuasion; however, because of how important it is, it needs to be reiterated. When people come to the negotiation table, they come with their beliefs, mindsets, and attitudes. Now, sometimes, these beliefs or mindsets do not favor you, and this means you have to change them through persuasion.

  The mindsets or beliefs do not even have to be about the negotiation or the issue at hand. Sometimes they are about you, and you can use persuasion to change the way the other party views you.

  For example, a former negotiation with an earlier client earned you a bad reputation in the industry or the status of a shrewd business person who everyone should be wary of when transacting business. Now, when people have to do business with you, they are careful and always on the defense so much that the negotiation process rarely goes smoothly. With persuasion, you can convince the client that the bad reputation is false. You can influence them to stop being on the defense, and you will end up having a smooth negotiation process and getting the best possible outcome.

- **Dispute management:** Paul is at a negotiation between the IT company he works at and a prospective client. A tactless colleague at the meeting has just said something the prospective client finds really annoying. Tempers are flaring; words are being exchanged.

Paul decides to step in and do something. At the office, he is known as a tension diffuser who is able to influence people to do his bidding. He calmly speaks to the client and then to his colleague. Apologies are exchanged, and everyone goes back to doing what they were doing earlier.

Sometimes, deals do not go through because they are open or latent disputes or rising tensions, and the two parties have gotten to a point where their judgment is clouded by their emotions. It takes the skill of persuasion to handle this and ensure that everyone goes back to the negotiation table and the deal is made.

This benefit of persuasion is particularly important because you should build relationships that leave room for further negotiation and business transactions after the initial negotiation.

- **Greater sales:** Stella is a businesswoman looking to sell her products. However, she is experiencing a drought. There is the problem of competitors who have established brands in the industry getting most of the patronage. Stella wants customers to patronize her business. She wants customers to buy her products. Not only is Stella looking for new customers who have not purchased a similar product, but she is also hoping to get some of her competitors' customers. She needs to convince these customers to buy her products.

When you are promoting your product or service to a customer, your ability to persuade them why they should patronize you is a vital part of you making any successful sale. You need to be able to convince your target market that you understand their needs and you know how to provide great solutions for those needs.

Persuasion during sales will help you show the customer the merits of giving you their money. Persuasion is important for negotiating even the price that will be paid by the customer. If you want to make a sales deal happen, learn how to be persuasive.

- **Career Advancement:** Everyone wants to grow. Career advancement also involves some negotiation. From negotiating your salary to negotiating with the management of the firm you work for a promotion and a pay raise, you need to have good negotiation skills to get your desired outcome.

When it comes to getting your desired outcome in terms of advancing your career, persuasion plays a significant role. If you already work at a firm and you would like to take on more responsibility, you would like to be promoted or you want a pay raise, you need to convince the management of the firm to get the desired outcome.

One good thing about persuasion is that its effects are not limited to a single person. You can use it to large audiences. If you are trying to pitch a product or service to a room full of potential investors, beyond persuading one person to invest in the product, you can persuade all the potential investors to make you great offers.

After discovering how persuasion can be beneficial to you, you should learn the types of persuasion. Learning the types of persuasion is a step in the right direction when it comes to learning how to wield persuasion as a valuable skill while negotiating.

Chapter 2:
History of Persuasion

H istorically, persuasion is rooted in ancient Greek's model of a prized politician and orator. To make the list, a politician or orator needs to master the use of rhetoric and elocution in other to persuade the public. Rhetoric according to Aristotle is the "ability to make use of the available methods of persuasion" to win a court case or influence the public during important orations. On the other hand, elocution (a branch of rhetoric), is the art of speech delivery which may include proper diction, proper gestures, stance and dress.

Persuasion in the business domain refers to a corporate system of influence aimed at changing another person groups, or organization's attitude, behavior or perception about an idea, object, goods, services or people.

It often employs verbal communications (both written and spoken), non-verbal communication (paralinguistic, chronemics, proxemics and so on), visual communication or a multimodal communication in order to convey, change or reinforce a piece of existing information or reasoning peculiar to the audience. Persuasion in business comes in different forms depending upon the need of the management.

For instance, a business enterprise sometimes uses persuasion in public relations, broadcast, media relations, speech writing, social media, customer-client relations, employee communication, and brand management.

Persuasion in psychological parlance refers to the use of an obtainable understanding of the social, behavioral, or cognitive principles of psychology to influence the attitude, cognition, behavior or belief system of a person, group or organization. It is also seen as a process by which the attitude and behavior of a person are influenced without any form of coercion but through the simple means of communication. For instance, when a child begs his mother for candy, and the mother refuses but instead offers a better food for the child to eat while also encouraging him that it will make him grow bigger.

The child gets excited and goes for the new alternative. In this way, the mother has been able to tap into his belief system without duress. Hence, persuasion can be used as a method of social control.

The verbal, non-verbal and visual forms of communication are manipulated just for the sole purpose of persuading an individual, group, or organization. Although communication is the most important and versatile form in which persuasion is manifested, it is worthy of note that not all forms of communication are intended to persuade. For instance, the celebration of a newly inaugurated president or governor circulated on the news cannot be classified as persuasion unless it is intended to impact the citizens of the country to react in certain ways.

Persuasion on its own is a branch of communication and popular as a method of social control, so it is worthy of note that not all forms of communication are intended to be persuasive. Other factors also determine a person's change in behavior or attitude; for example, verbal threats, a person's current psychological state, physical coercion, etc.

While discussing the various meanings of persuasion, it can be observed that persuasion extends beyond a specific field to different areas of study. However, communication and psychology are clearly used for persuasion to take place.

While communication provides the model for how interlocutors in the art of persuasion get their messages understood, psychology provides the model for the mental processes used during persuasion.

Chapter 3:
Principles of Persuasion

T he psychology of persuasion is based on six principles:

- Scarcity
- Reciprocity
- Sympathy and like-ability
- Authority
- Commitment and consistency
- Social proof

Reciprocity

We are compelled by social norms to react to favor and respond with another favor. We do that naturally so we do not seem ungrateful. Initiating a favor can result in so many reciprocations of the favor in the future. This principle is widely applied in sales and marketing, where free samples and giveaways are used to initiate transactions. When using the principle of reciprocity to influence others, it is good to be careful.

Consistency and Commitment

There is a tendency in every human being to want to appear consistent with want we have bought, what we have said, and what we've done. We feel the pressure to follow our prior commitments when making new decisions. For example, you can keep old customers with ease as you attract new ones.

Commitment is fueled by the desire to appear like someone

consistent in behavior and attitude over time. We are more likely to consistently go through a plan after we commit to it publicly. For example, let's say that you have five restaurants to order a meal. You call three of them to order supper- for three different types of food. By the time you pass by each restaurant to collect your food, you find that only one has prepared the food well and is ready; but for others, you have to wait for thirty more minutes. The chances are high that next time when you need the same service, you will not call the two restaurants where you were delayed for thirty minutes. You will feel compelled to call the one that came through because you think they will be consistent in their commitment to serve you well.

Social Proof

At any given moment, you rely on what others are doing to make your decision, and you will find yourself choosing the almost full restaurant. To be accepted by society or social subgroups, we tend to act in the same way as our community, even if it is wrong. We tend to follow trends, and marketers have mastered the art of harnessing the power of social proof.

Sympathy/ Likeability

If someone you love wants or asks you to do something, you are more likely to do it. Even something as superficial as the physical appearance of someone can influence you to do something for them. When you like someone, you want to reflect well on them. If the people you like is doing something, you want to be part of doing it because you want to be associated with the person. You will be influenced to support a cause that your family, colleague, and friends also support. Companies use this principle with great success when they send sale agents into their communities. It is more likely that people will buy from those who are like them, i.e., people they know and respect or friends. Sympathy is, therefore, key to influencing buyers. People will rarely buy something from someone they don't like.

When you reflect someone else's behavior, such as dressing in a way that aligns with their interests, speaking the same language, or copying their body language, they will like and sympathize with you.

Authority

People tend to believe people with authority or someone they trust and respect. The ordinary individual will accept what is being said by any individual showing authority - without questioning it. A figure of authority can be a politician, a celebrity, or any other local hero well known to the people. You can influence people by using a figure of authority to deliver your message, other than having to do it yourself.

In general, people tend to obey authority figures, regardless of whether those authority figures are questionable. It is human nature. That is why companies use persons with authority to advertise their goods. The opinion of such professionals and experts is critical and acts as a testimony to guide customers who are not sure about a purchase.

Scarcity

People want something more when they realize that its supply is low. When there is a perception that something is limited, it is the nature of human beings to want it more. To buy something when it is the very last one or where a perception has been created that the special expires soon is a common human behavior. Businesses use such techniques to make huge sales within a short period of time. When customers or supporters get wind of limited stock or few tickets to an upcoming event, or just a few positions remain to be filled, they get a feeling that they might miss out and so they act quickly to secure their item or positions.

Elements of Persuasion

The first element of persuasion is often symbolic. Persuasion utilizes words, sounds, as well as images to get the message across to the "victim". The logic behind this is quite simple.

The second element is that persuasion is used deliberately to affect how others act or think. This one is quite obvious; you don't use persuasion to get someone to change if you don't deliberately try to affect them. To get the person to believe the same way they do, the persuader will attempt distinct strategies.

The distinctive thing about persuasion is that it enables some type of free will. In this way, the buyer is permitted to create his or her own decision. For the most part, they don't have to go for it, no matter how hard somebody tries to persuade them. The subject might hear about the best car to buy in a thousand commercials, but if they don't like that brand or don't need a new vehicle, they won't buy it.

Examples of persuasion can be found everywhere, including when you talk to individuals you know, on the Internet, on the radio and television. It is also feasible to deliver persuasive messages by nonverbal and verbal means, although when verbal methods are used, it is much more efficient.

The ability to influence someone during a conversation and make a decision is necessary to become one of the most important people in the world today. This ability is useful in business negotiations, and in everyday life.

In general, the impact on people is not so obvious. The basic idea is that people's behavior is often guided by their subconscious desires. To achieve your goals, you need to understand these simple desires and then make your target passionately wish for something.

People often use psychology to manipulate others. Even in ancient times when priests ruled the people, instilling religion was harsh, and everyone would be punished if they did follow the established rules and practices. Psychological influence strongly acts on the subconscious, causing the victim to be led by a skilled manipulator.

You will grow your personality only when in close cooperation with a community. From childhood, we develop the basic patterns of behavior and outlook produced by the historical, biological and mental development of humankind. To have influence and control over another person, you must know their personality and behavioral traits. Most importantly, you must learn how to master the specific methods and techniques of influence on outlook, character, personality type and other important psychological features.

To help people to look beyond the limits of consciousness, professionals use a variety of methods of direct influence on the psyche, whose essence consists of a narrowed state of consciousness, making it is easy to control someone. Persuasion may involve the use of powerful symbolic words like freedom, justice, and equality, and nonverbal visual signs such as the holy cross, and the flag, and familiar images. Such symbols are the tools of the persuader to drive attitudes and mold opinions.

Chapter 4:
Difference between Manipulation and Persuasion

M any people fail to recognize the nuances that exist between manipulation and persuasion. Despite the fact that both seek to convince someone to do something, they are quite different in enough ways to be classified completely differently. One is only beneficial to the manipulator (manipulation) while the other, ideally, should benefit both people. Because of these key differences, manipulation is far more insidious than persuasion. The manipulator sees the other person as a tool and a means to an end, whereas the persuader sees the other person as a partner.

Defining Persuasion

Though persuasion involves changing the mind of someone else, it is not necessarily a bad thing—there are plenty of ways that persuasion can be used innocently or benevolently. Persuasion is any method that actively changes the thoughts, emotions, actions, or attitudes of another. It can be done inwardly through changing one's own attitudes, or it can be done to other people.

Persuasion is used as a form of influence—it is everywhere. It is present in ads, politics, schools, professions, and just about everywhere you could think of. When persuading someone, there are four key elements that must be present:

- Someone who is doing the persuading
- The message or the persuasion

- A target recipient for the persuasion
- A context that the persuasion is received

Each of these four elements must be present for something to be considered persuasive. Of course, this means that manipulation would fall within the category of persuasion as well.

Defining Manipulation

In psychology, manipulation is a type of influence or persuasion, but unlike regular persuasion, manipulation is covert, deceptive, or underhanded. This means that, unlike regular persuasion, which seeks to be most honest, manipulation is often untrustworthy.

The manipulator seeks only to further serve himself, and he does not care about the target and about hurting the target. The target is seen as little more than collateral damage—a necessary sacrifice to get the desired results. As such, manipulation tactics are oftentimes quite exploitative and almost always meant to be insidious and harmful.

Successful manipulation requires three key concepts to happen:

- Concealing intentions and behaviors while remaining friendly upfront
- Understanding the ways the victim or target is vulnerable and using those vulnerabilities to the advantage of the manipulator
- Being ruthless enough not to care about the harm caused to the victim

Manipulation can take several different forms, but most of them follow the pattern of being covert, harmful, and causing no guilt to the manipulator.

Key Differences

Ultimately, persuasion and manipulation are quite similar: They are both forms of social influence, but that is where the similarities end. While persuasion is generally positive, even within dark psychology, manipulation is not. Manipulation is harmful, ruthless, and insidious in every way, shape, and form.

When trying to decide whether something is manipulative or persuasive, there are a few questions you can ask yourself. This simple test allows you to analyze what you are doing and saying to ensure you are making the choices that work best for you. If you are not looking to manipulate, but the questions tell you that you are erring on the side of manipulation, you know to tone it down a bit and lighten up on the manipulative factors:

- What intention has led you to feel the need to convince the other person of something?
- Are you being truthful about your intention and the process?
- How does this benefit the other person?

The persuader is going to be attempting to convince the other person from a good place—they want to help the other person somehow. While they may benefit too, they are primarily looking out for the other person's best interest. For example, you may try to convince someone to buy a specific car because it will work better for their family than the car the person is currently looking at. This would be seen as persuasion as you are offering facts about the other car and showing how it would likely serve longer and better.

On the other hand, when the manipulator is not concerned with the needs of the other person, the manipulator is going to attempt to push for whatever benefits him or her the most. There is no good intention here nor much truth. It is also not likely to benefit the other person at all, and may even be detrimental. For example, the manipulator may try to sell a car that is no good for the buyer simply because the other car may be worth more money and therefore net a much higher commission. The car is not likely to be very good for what the buyer needs, but that is not the manipulator's concern. The manipulator would see that as something the buyer should know on his own so there is no reason to bother pointing out the ways that the buyer may be making a bad decision, even if the manipulator knows the decision is wrong.

Chapter 5:
Methods of Persuasion

I n terms of the process of persuasion, there will usually be three parts to follow, including the communicator or the medium used as the source of persuasion

The Persuasive Nature of the Appeal

This is about good persuasion and using the right techniques.

Foot in the door

This one allows you to ask for a bigger favor after you have already been granted a smaller favor, especially if they are related in some way. You may start off with something pretty small, such as borrowing a cup of sugar from your neighbor. Your neighbor will probably be fine with this because it's not that big of a deal and most people, as long as they have it on hand, will have a cup of sugar to share with you.

Reversal tagging

Another option is known as reversal tagging. This is a trick that uses simple and subtle sentence phrasing to get to an agreement, or at least compliance, from the target in general. It will use two opposing structures inside the sentence, the first part being an affirmative statement and the second will be a tag question.

Reverse psychology

This is a principle that can work well with those who like to have control, such as rebellious people or those who just like to do the opposite of what they are told to do.

Counter-attitudinal advocacy

It is pretty common for people to state a view on something, or even to support an opinion, even if that is not something they believe themselves. This isn't necessarily that deceptive because the things that people choose to do are usually small or have the best intentions. For example, it is common for someone to tell a little white lie because it will help to protect the feelings of someone else. When this happens, we are attempting to reduce the dissonance we caused by saying that our actions are still noble.

Perceived self-interest

If you ask anyone, they often say they are generous and pretty caring creatures. No matter how much most people believe this, though, as humans we are a self-serving species. The idea behind this technique is a pretty simple one, but you will be spending your time on perception. If you can convince your target that they are doing something in their best interest, whether true or not, then the target is much more likely to go along with the whole scheme. This can be apparent when you are trying to persuade someone who is higher up than you.

Hurt and rescue principle

This principle is based on evoking some discomfort or fear in the person from the start. You need to be able to manufacture a level of discomfort first and crafty enough because making this work can be hard.

Trial ballooning

Another option is known as trial is ballooning or trial closing. This is the starting point, and it is relevant whether you are the seller or the buyer in the negotiation. The idea is to start out with the final solution you would like to end up with. You just put the information out there and see if the tactic works.

Auction model

This strategy is good to put in place if you are working with more than one buyer at the same time. Otherwise, it won't be the best one. With this method, you want to play one of the parties against the others so there is a buying frenzy, and it is more likely that the price will be driven up - no matter what you are trying to sell.

Chapter 6:
Subliminal Persuasion

S ubliminal persuasion is a term mostly found in advertisement. It's often associated with the idea of tricking someone into picking up a message without their awareness. The persuasion is done on a level that those being persuaded can't initially, or easily, pick up on.

It is yet another manipulative tactic that many people use on those around them. Subliminal persuasion isn't as invasive or harmful as other forms of manipulation, but it can still be dangerous. Of all the other forms of manipulation, this might be one of the hardest to detect as well.

The idea of subliminal persuasion is that its influences are below the detectable conscious human level. Those who are being subliminally manipulated won't be able to realize what's going on until it's far too late. In some cases of manipulation, one can recognize it while it's happening. But for the most part, many people can go years before they realize that they were subliminally persuaded.

The Subconscious Mind

Our subconscious mind works so much harder than our conscious one. It pretty much never shuts off and is constantly making decisions for us before we even realize what's going on. Even while we rest our conscious mind, our subconscious one is putting on various movies for us in the form of dreams. The subconscious has so much information that it has to create delusions, daydreams, and other forms of dissociation to process all that it knows.

The human brain is pretty much limitless. There might actually be a limit to how many things we can know, but we haven't found the number quite yet. We've made assumptions on how far we think our brains can go. Even though we basically pack information into our brains all day, never feeling like we know too much, most of us will just use what we have already.

The subconscious is powerful. It consumes about 95% of our brains, yet we don't have complete control over it. Our subconscious mind could be why we develop certain fears or have certain addictions. For every time you felt as if you didn't know why you were having a certain thought or emotion, there's a good chance your subconscious brain knew exactly why.

Your subconscious mind has been working the whole time you've been slacking off! Remember that one time you stayed up all night to study for a test? You might not have a specific recollection of that night, but your subconscious does. It's what's reminding you to get your work done on time so you don't have to endure the pain you felt the day after pulling an all-nighter ever again.

The key to most of our conscious issues lies directly in our subconscious. Why might a person think that dogs are scary? They usually look to their subconscious mind and realize that they internalized something dark in their past to make them fearful of dogs.

We'll never be fully aware of our subconscious or the way it works, but that doesn't mean we shouldn't try. The more we can understand the innerworkings of our brains, the better we'll be at fixing them in the long run.

Subliminal Advertising

Subliminal advertising uses our subconscious against us. It sneaks certain thoughts, feelings, and emotions into the things we consume in order to buy into products more and more. Some countries have even banned subliminal advertising, knowing just how dangerous this manipulation tactic can be.

Advertisers know how to get into our heads, literally. They sometimes even pay people to watch their advertisements while their brain function is monitored to get an idea of how the brain works while watching advertisements. They'll even track eye movement to see what part of the commercial are being studied. All this information is then used against us to specifically sell something.

Social Media

Social media has seemingly taken over the lives of many people. Not only do people create social media for themselves, but they make pages for their dogs as well! Social media isn't all bad, but it's agreeably inescapable.

The people you follow on social media are likely using subliminal persuasion without you even realizing it. They can alter what the world sees of their lives, using pictures, quotes, videos, and other small glimpses into themselves. We see more than we would see in any other context, so we start using this as our identifying factors for a specific person. Many people still keep in touch with those on social media that they haven't spoken to in a decade. Their in-person perception has faded and now all that exists is who they are as a social media personality.

Many users see the happy face of a baby, but they don't see that the same baby had puked all over its mom and the new white rug once the camera was turned off.

This manipulation makes many people feel less than themselves. They feel inadequate after comparing themselves to the people online that are living so happily. Many use this form of subliminal persuasion to make themselves feel better. And it works!

Chapter 7:
Ways to Become Extremely Persuasive

Ｎone of us is born being the best negotiator. Although we negotiate innocuously in our day-to-day lives, we need to learn some important strategies so we can take our negotiations skills to the following level. These strategies could be equally effective in getting work done by your kids as well as in closing a coveted business deal. Basically, when you are an amazing negotiator, you are sure of receiving only the best deals. Let's get started with the strategies to use in shaping you to become the best negotiator.

#1 Creating a Lull

While negotiations are in process, do not give in to haste and speed. Rather, take a slight pause so that a lull is created in the whole discussion. There may be several attractions and giveaways from the opponents' sides. Do not rush into them. Taking a break will show your independent demeanor and allow you to negotiate freely and without any psychological baggage. Don't be too quick to give in to what your opponent is offering. Take your time to always evaluate your options to know if you can still get a better deal than what is being offered.

#2 Being Mr. /Ms. Know It All

Having adequate information before venturing into negotiation is a useful strategy. While you will get ample time to gather your wits and ideas, your opponents will take it as your silent signal for being unsatisfied. Who knows, this pause could be just what you need to strike that deal. Never show your opponent that you are not aware of certain information even if you don't know since they will use your weakness to emerge victorious in the negotiations.

#3 Put on Your Opponent's Shoes

There are situations where many complicated and high-end strategies fail and the best way to get on track is to simply understand your opponent's point. This will help you even know their following step before they even put it forward during the negotiations.

#4 Exude Self-belief

One of the well-known killers of negotiations is desperation. However desperate you may be to clinch the deal or situation, do not let your opposition get to see it. Instead, exude great self-belief and even be confident enough to walk away during the discussions. Your self-belief will safeguard your fears from being sensed by opposing negotiators lest they take advantage of them.

#5 Splitting the Difference

This classic and safe strategy encourages amiability right from the beginning. Many negotiators spilt the differences fairly so that both the parties get equated benefits. Fair individuals who believe in setting an equitable deal or arrangement usually adopt this tactic. This strategy is akin to compromising and the opponent is treated akin to an associate and not a competitor. This is strategy is very helpful especially when you need to offer a solution and walking away is not an option.

10 Ways to be Persuasive

Being a good negotiator may not necessarily mean that you are persuasive. Being persuasive is the #1 strategy to be the top negotiator who gets his or her way. Even if you use these strategies, you cannot be the top negotiator if you are not persuasive. In fact, without persuasion, negotiation will lose its steam and would be like an ordinary discussion wherein one would agree and the other one will disagree.

From being persuasive to believing in yourself and being able to persuade your opponent that what you are offering is the best deal possible, persuasion is necessary during negotiations. Persuasion takes place in our lives involuntarily most of the time. We are persuasive in varying degrees while playing our multiple roles of a professional, friend, spouse, and parent or as a shopper.

Here are 10 ways to be more persuasive:

#1 Start on an Agreeable Note

If you want to sell your point of view, buy into their version first. Starting on an agreeable note has always rendered positive results. This strategy works psychologically as you are likely to gain several points in the mind of opponents, and they become receptive to what you have to say.

#2 Be purposeful

Being purposeful will give you a reason to be persuasive. While kids can be persuasive without any logical reason, and it suits them well, grownups often hold themselves back until they have some valid reason to persuade others. When you have a purpose, you will be more confident in your tone and demeanor.

#3 Be a Good Listener

You need to understand that persuasion is totally different from pushing. Thus, listening is an integral part of being a good persuader. Those who keep on ranting and just believe in drilling their words into others often get nowhere. Be persuasive by being articulate in speaking as well as listening. The key to persuade effectively is to know others' version and taking their argument in your style.

#4 Create Bonds and Connections

Smart persuaders do not leave out emotions or feelings. They suavely establish relevant and appealing bonds and connections that consequently work in their favor. This ability places them in a likable league, and they are heard with better attention and inclination. Persuade others patiently and with empathy giving no space to rashness or impatience. This way, it is going to be much easier indeed.

#5 Reinforce Credibility

To be persuasive in real and effective sense, do not beat around the bush laying stress over facts. It is to be understood that sometimes mere "black-and-white" perceptions get ruled out and subjectivity has to be roped in to influence others. Make a point to highlight and reinforce the strong point and credibility of others simply because you want the same from others. Giving respect and credibility to others will make them more receptive to your point of view.

#6 Offer Agreement

Persuasion is not about winning by hook-or-by-crook like a war. Effectual persuaders underline the belief that they don't have to win every negotiation. Rather, they are intelligent enough to backtrack as the situation demands. They think creatively and sometimes offer agreement by meeting the solution midway. It is all about giving in when you have scope and holding on when it matters.

#7 Know when to Keep Quiet

Strategic persuaders hardly beat around the bush with their verbosity. They know when to shut their mouths so their presented arguments can work on others' minds. After driving your final point, just relax your vocal cords and let it work for you.

#8 Talk Swift to Corner Skeptics

If your opponents are known skeptics, be a swift and smooth talker. This will hamper their thought processes, and they would find it tough to find loopholes in your point of view. Your rapid talk will be associated with expertise, intensity and confidence.

#9 Limit the Choices

According to conventional thinking, "choices leverage the chances". However, this becomes paradoxical in the case of persuasion. The more options or choices offered, the more the chances of persuading go down.

#10 Repeated Drilling

Though kids resort to such a persuasion technique, planned and tactical drilling can have some desired effect. Repetition plays with human minds, and it starts contemplating the concept, sometimes even subconsciously.

After discussing all these persuasion tricks, it is important to convey that these should not be applied blatantly or desperately. They work best when applied proficiently. Overdoing them renders bleak results, as no one is dumb enough not to ever get the negative feelers up. Your need to persuade your opponent proves they are not witless about what is already known.

Chapter 8:
Influencing People

The following points will make it easier to influence persons with authority:

1. Conduct Research to Identify the Person's Achievements

Persons in authority love it when juniors humor their egos a bit. Therefore, take to the internet and get to know all that your employer, professor or pastor has done. Carefully study his professional history and see the people he or she knows in your current field or in the area you hope to get into in the future. Read the files the person has authored and if possible, source the person's theses and research to know more about the things they are passionate about. The knowledge you get will be excellent jumping off points and will show the authority figure that you did your homework.

2. Be Prepared

While it is essential to know the interests of the person you will be speaking with, know that flattery and knowing their backgrounds will only help you build rapport; but what will get them interested in you and in what you are saying are the concepts and new information you intend to discuss. If you want to ask a question about the content you are learning in a class, ensure that you have read through the assigned reading and done the assignments issued.

Even if you want to speak to someone on a different matter, you might be surprised to see your professor asking class-related questions, and this will require you to be well-read and prepared on these matters too. You are not going to "wing it" since this situation needs preparation on all fronts.

3.   Be Practical

It is very irresponsible to wait around for the problem to become worse just because you were scared of speaking to a supervisor, your professor, or any other person in a position of authority. If you wait too long, the authority figure may become disappointed and might not treat you with as much kindness and sympathy. He will find you are irresponsible for allowing the problem to progress so much, and you could lose your job, be forced to repeat your class, or face any other negative outcome. Therefore, at the first sign of trouble, schedule a meeting with the authority figure and get them to resolve the problem early on.

4.   Be Respectful

Our upbringings and the hierarchies in society have conditioned us to address people differently, according to their relative authority. Therefore, ensure you show respect to authority figures. However, do not talk to seniors sycophantically with phrases like "to be honest", and "with all due respect" because they sound condescending.

On the other hand, do not let senior people silence you or dominate the conversation. There is always a temptation to shut people up or keep quiet and let the opinions of authority figures take the day, even when they are erroneous. However, if you are continually taking orders without considering your thoughts, the executives will not respect you either. The best way is to present your best ideas, and if you need to correct authority figures, do so respectfully.

When addressing your juniors, accord them the same respect you give to seniors. Be attentive to what they say, acknowledge their views, and add onto their ideas when the opportunity presents itself. Forcing your opinions or communicating with them forcefully is a sign of disrespect. If you genuinely believe that your opinion is better, give it to them respectfully and allow them to take up your idea themselves, having seen that it is better. Let the decision be theirs.

5.   Be Willing to Challenge Them

Experts who have interviewed various leaders from different spheres of life report that the leaders often say that they value the kind of thoughtful input that creates an engaging debate. It would be boring if all people followed their bosses' opinions. However, an atmosphere in which people challenge each other and present contrary views promotes growth and creative thinking. That's the reason why leaders look for unique talent; they want diverse creative ideas because that is what gives their companies a competitive edge.

When you present your critical thoughts to the table, ensure that you do it in a way that invites discussion, critique, and collaboration. Approaching issues in this way will yield more productive results rather than having a combative dialogue or just staying quiet.

While you should keep in mind the above points when relating to people in authority, the issue at hand and the relationship you have with the authority figure matters. Always remember the role that the authority individual plays in your life and the havoc it would wreak if you were at odds with that person.

Sycophancy comes off as being "thirsty" and insincere; therefore, only be polite and respectful. Maintain an upright posture, make direct eye contact, and speak confidently in your normal voice. If you are meeting the individual for the first time, let your handshake be firm, but don't overdo it. While you may want to impress, do not smile too often or excessively. Do not nod too much. Be likable and ensure that your manners are proper. Your goal, when speaking to an authority figure, should not be to get them to like you; it would be better if they respected you because they will come to trust and depend on you.

If you are asked questions, such as in a traffic stop, answer the questions briefly and truthfully. Address the police officer respectfully by referring to the person as sir or madam, but don't overdo it lest you sound insincere.

How to Put Your View Across to Someone in Authority

While the traditional hierarchical leadership setup is disappearing from the corporate sector as many organizations open up opportunities for employees to lead and contribute their ideas freely, the reality of superiority and power has not disappeared. In fact, juniors are still expected to honor those ahead of them in power and treat them with respect. Your boss may be open to having meals with you, playing games with you, engaging in discussions, and other forms of socialization outside the work environment. However, despite the cordial relationship, keep in mind that he or she is in a position of power and they could influence the direction of your career.

Here are tips to help you steer out of trouble areas as you engage with your bosses and other persons in authority in society:

1.   Be Resolute in Regards To Your Convictions

Sharing your ideas with others always seems like an uphill task, especially when the persons in questions are colleagues you esteem, people outside your team or persons in authority like bosses, prospective clients, police officers, and senior executives. The idea of sharing your opinion in itself might make you feel like you are going over your head. However, if you don't share your opinion, how will they know? How will they know that you have something useful to bring to the table? You must muster courage and indicate that you have something to contribute.

2.   Avoid Sitting on The Fence

Sitting on the fence in regard to your ideas refers to being undecided about whether the ideas or the points you want to present are worthwhile. Undecided opinions start with words like, "I'm not sure that this idea will work, but we should give it a try," or "I'm sorry if you are already aware of this but..." In cases like this, your modesty could be taken as uncertainty. Avoid starting your statements with words like, "I might be wrong..." or "I guess that could work..." or "It could be that..."

With every conversation you have with superiors, you reaffirm their decision to hire you. Therefore, when you speak, don't begin planting doubts in their minds, making them wonder whether they were right to hire you.

3.   Defend Your Ideas

It may turn out that in some instances, you will have to defend your ideas. Explaining and defending your view can be tough, especially if you have to defend them against contradictory ideas raised by persons in authority. However, be strong and engage them because the ideas worth sharing - the kind likely to bring transformation - will be controversial to some point.

4. Challenge Other People

In the same way as other people challenge your ideas, test theirs too. This is not done on a revenge mission, but it allows you to explore an idea and examine it from all possible angles before implementing it. By asking questions, you and the others listening will also get clarity on the issue at hand; and from there, you can even come up with better ideas than the one being presented.

5. Have an Open Mind

You cannot control how other people think and respond to your ideas, but you can control the reaction you give, whatever response you get. It often takes an open mind.

Chapter 9:
Conversational Skills Techniques

D o you wish you could have a conversation with a person you have never met before and they will automatically like you? Think about people who seem to always bring the best out of you. You feel comfortable talking with them, and you could continue talking with them forever. They could be somebody you have known your whole life or somebody you have just met, but the conversation flows naturally and smoothly.

If you wish you could have this natural ability, don't worry. There are ways to give it to you. You can be in control of a conversation and gain the interest of others. While we may use the word control, we don't mean that you are the one continually talking and "controlling" everything. We suggest you know how to work on a conversation so that it continues naturally. The essential factors in a good conversation are active listening, showing curiosity, and keeping sarcasm to a minimum. But to give you a good start, here are a few conversation skills techniques:

Make the Conversation About the Other Person

Have you ever had the issue of conversation with somebody who went on and on about something that you didn't have the slightest interest in? You likely felt wiped out by the end of the conversation, and it probably felt like they were talking to themselves. They are oblivious to the idea that you might not be interested in what they like.

The best conversations tend to be the ones that show an interest in the listener, their interests, and their world. Most people like to talk about themselves. Take the time to ask them an open-ended question about something you may have noticed. If you make sure to give them positive feedback or a sincere compliment, you will have made a great start. Conversationalists are sincerely interested in other people, take the time to notice things, and use that information to fuel and start their conversations.

Take the Conversation Deeper

Think about the people in your life that you are most willing to open yourself up to and share things with them. What about them makes you comfortable disclosing personal things that you wouldn't typically tell others?

More than likely, they always make eye contact, and they make you feel as if you are getting their full attention. Please pay attention to the expressions they make. Notice how they are entirely with you, not only what they say but in their facial expressions. They look happy when you share something you are excited or happy about. They will look solemn when you share something sad. You can feel that they are entirely into everything you are saying.

If trying to emulate what they do seems unnatural, continue to practice and push yourself until you have learned how. You will start to notice that other people will react differently when talking with you.

Ask Them Good Questions

You can get other people to share more by showing that you are interested in asking questions. It will help the conversation to move deeper. Some good questions ask them how they feel or think about something they have been talking about. If you have had a conversation recently, bring up something from the last conversation. More than likely, if they bring up something, it is an interest and essential. Take a moment to think about other areas connected to the interests you know they have and what they might like to talk about.

Take into Consideration the Time and Space

Don't bring a conversation beyond pleasantries unless you know that you have time to listen to the person. Places that are loud with many other people aren't the best to get into a good conversation. To have a good conversation, you need a quiet and relaxed environment without a bunch of pressure and distractions. Coffee shops are good for conversations. Sports bars aren't.

Show Curiosity

Having a real conversation means that you have created a space for understanding. Real conversations give you a place for learning, and it helps to promote the deepening and nurturing of relationships. The essential of all is that honest conversations feed our souls in ways that many other things can't.

So, improving your ability to grow, maintain, and create real conversations is a skill that needs to be practiced, whether you are coming from it as a friend, spouse, child, colleague, or parent. One habit that can help you nurture a real conversation in any area of your life is curiosity.

Curiosity tends to be associated with children or highly creative adults. But curiosity is an essential and fundamental quality needed for anybody interested in lifelong learning. There are four areas in conversations that curiosity helps with.

When curious, we ask questions. Alright, who are the most curious humans on Earth? Kids. What is that they do ad nauseam? Ask questions. What is it that will keep interactions with others from developing into a conversation? No questions.

When you have a conversation and say something, and they say something but no questions are asked, you might experience an exchange, but it doesn't go much deeper than that. If you want to stimulate the conversation, don't just create points and opinions instead of creating questions about things you would like to learn. If you ever start feeling like you are talking too much, shift the conversation, and ask them a question.

When curious, we listen to the answers. Asking questions may be necessary, but having a barrage of questions thrown at you can feel like an inquisition. What takes us from an inquiry to a conversation is that you shut up and listen after you ask a question. If you want to learn the answer, you will listen to their response because you want to know. The main reason why real conversations can improve relationships is that they require a person to listen actively.

When curious, we are interested. Curiosity drives interest. Think about classes you did well in a while in school and those you didn't. What was the difference? We guess that you found some interesting and others, not so much. Being interested makes you want to learn more. It happens with conversations as well. When you are interested in the conversation, asking questions and listening to their answers, it gets more comfortable.

When curious, we want to learn. When you are ready to learn, you put yourself in place to engage in conversation for learning, not just feeling like you have to get through it.

With these four things; questions, listening, interest, and a desire to learn, you can create a conversation and get all of the benefits from it.

Active Listening

Since we listen so much, you would think that we are amazing at it. Most people aren't, and research suggests that most people only remember around 25 to 50 percent of everything they hear. It means that when you have a conversation with your significant other for about ten minutes, they are paying attention to less than half of what is being said.

If you flip this around, it also means that you don't hear the full message when given directions. You hope that the essential parts are held within that 25-50 percent, but what happens if they weren't?

Listening is something that everybody needs to improve. When you become a better listener, you will also see improvement in your productivity, influence, and negotiation. What's more, you will be able to avoid conflict and other misunderstandings.

You can't become distracted by whatever else may be happening around you or by thinking about what you will say next. You also got to make sure that you stay engaged so you don't end up losing focus. To enhance your listening skills, you have to let the other person know that you are listening to what is being said.

Sarcasm

There are people in everyone's life who love to use little sarcastic and passive-aggressive modes of communication. They think their sarcasm is well-meaning, but based on research, sarcasm is thinly veiled meanness. Sarcasm is a way to cover up hate or contempt. It is a quick way to ruin a conversation, as well. But why do people use sarcasm?

Sarcasm does not only tend to be hurtful, but it is one of the least natural forms of communication. You must watch the things you say. Sarcasm isn't funny because it usually involves hurting another person. It isn't going to improve a relationship or lighten the mood. There are other fun ways to lighten the mood, but picking on a person, which is what you are doing, isn't going to help. You will lose respect if you continuously use sarcasm.

To control and maintain a real conversation, make sure you remember these three essential things: show curiosity, actively listen, and cut out the sarcasm.

Chapter 10:
Using Humor in Persuasion

Humor has a number of benefits for persuasion and communication. When you desire to communicate better and faster, you need to inject some humor in your conversation. Additionally, you need to understand as well as appreciate humor from all angles. Using humor allows you to create content that is more memorable and permits you to generate interest, get attention, and even encourage action.

To get humor across to the audience, you need to understand the mood of the people you are communicating with. When used the right way, humor represents an excellent tool for persuasion. If you have watched television for a long time, surely you can remember an ad that made you laugh your head off and yet you received the message. Years later, when you see the item in a supermarket, you remember the comic relief the ad used. This is the same way you need to use humor to make people get persuaded.

Many people remember something that made them smile, which usually leads to a purchasing decision. When you get someone in the right mood, you make them do anything you wish them to do. So, when you decide to persuade someone, take time to understand the mood of the person you are targeting before you start your persuasion.

On the other hand, if a person is in a bad mood, any attempt at being comical will result in disaster. Don't attempt to persuade them, instead choose another day when you can change their mood or find a way to uplift their mood before trying anything.

When it comes to persuasion, humor is useful since it helps you gain attention quickly, and it allows you to build rapport as well. The message you pass across becomes memorable, also relieving tension, decreasing stress level, and motivating them.

Humor should be Relevant

When using humor as a persuasion tool, make sure it is relevant to the topic. You can use humor in various stages of the conversation – to introduce the topic, build upon it, and then conclude.

Don't just use humor in a way that doesn't add to your goals. Make sure it makes a point or states a fact but in a humorous way because this will make your conversation more receptive to the listener.

When using humor, don't overdo it; otherwise, you will have a negative impact than the one you expected. The other party will look at you as irrelevant and ignore you, especially when they feel you are trying to be too funny when you need to be serious. Remember that you are trying to change the mood of the person and not trying to impress them.

The perception of humor is different across audiences and the world in general. This might limit the ability of your persuasiveness to be funny. It is ideal to do some research so you know which type of humor will be most useful in a situation.

Benefits of Humor in Persuasion

Persuasion is all about making the other person believe in what you are trying to get across. But for you to pass the message across the right way, you also need to be in the right frame of mind.

Here is how humor helps you persuade better:

- Humor helps lower your blood pressure.
- When you laugh, you exercise various muscles in your body, which makes you healthier.
- When you laugh along with others, you strengthen your immunity and decrease stress hormones.
- It also improves breathing in such a way that you can breathe deeper.
- Humor also distracts you from any negative emotions that might crop up.
- It also connects you to other people because audiences love happy people.
- It increases energy.

Types of Humor to Enhance Persuasion

Humor can take many forms, but sadly, many people don't stop to look at the type of humor they are using and categorize it. For you to know what type of humor to apply in persuasion, you need to understand the following types:

Anecdotal

These are personal stories that don't need any validation or statistics. Audiences across love funny stories, and when you use anecdotes, you need to make sure they are relevant, timely, and compelling. To make use of anecdotes, you need to make the short, brief, and real.

Self-Deprecating

This usually involves making fun of yourself. You make yourself the point of reference and show that you don't take yourself seriously. Use this humor to generate some laughs around the office, especially if you are known to be the serious person in the office. Just like any other humor, the more you make self-deprecating and spontaneous, the better.

Epigrammatic

This is an insightful statement that is brief and memorable. Make sure you have a few epigrammatic statements and then use them when the right time comes. You can use the epigrammatic humor to lighten the mood, as an icebreaker, or as relief from an awkward moment. You can use epigrammatic statements that have been used before or you can develop some of your own.

Irony

Irony represents a contrast between what is normal and what occurs. You can use irony to draw parallels in situations or use two images to show how irony works for you.

Satire

This is a kind of humor that looks at the shortcomings of a specific society, government, company, or people. It is usually regarded as a rough form of humor. It can take the form of satire, hyperbole, or parody. Just like when you use other types of humor, make sure you understand your audience well before you use satire because when one person misinterprets the parody as insubordination or poor attitude, you will end up running for damage control.

Deadpan

This is also referred to as dry humor, and it consists of a funny statement that is delivered in an insincere tone. You can use this in various situations, including meetings to conferences.

How to Use Humor to Your Advantage

While your sense of humor can create prospects for better persuasion, you need to make sure you know what to do. In fact, more than 70 percent of executives agree that humor makes persuasion easier. A comic touch helps you build rapport and relieves tension in a situation that is tough. It also makes you fun to be around. Before you use humor in persuasion, know the dos and don'ts of adding humor in persuasion.

Check the "Pulse" of the Audience

You need to identify the mood of the audience before you make the decision to use humor. If you are persuading employees in an established corporation, go with subtle humor, while more entrepreneurial environments can require you to use humor with an edge.

Try It Out

Before you can take your humor up the stage, you need to make sure that it works. Make sure you try out with your friends and family and see their reaction. If they look at you as if you are from another world, then drop it.

Don't Use a Series

Using humor to persuade is a great tool, but when it is successful, don't add more jokes. If a joke has been received well, thank your lucky stars. Remember, you don't want to look desperate in front of the audience.

Incorporate it Naturally

When using humor, make sure you use funny things that arise from real life. When used correctly, this kind of humor is easy to relate to and will help get the message home.

Avoid Offensive Humor

This is obvious because using a joke that is offensive can kill your delivery. While it can help you achieve the goal, it can still offend the audience and make you lose credibility. Avoid racist, ethnic, vulgar, sexist, and indecent humor; instead, keep it clean and straightforward.

Persuasive Listening

For many people, changing the other person's view means talking more than listening. You feel that when you speak more and more, the other person will listen. Often this is not the case, and many people end up failing to drive the point home just because they were unable to realize that listening is very persuasive.

Being silent allows the other person to tell you their position, whether a good or a bad one. If you are fond of shouting people down with the aim of forcing them to listen to your point of view, it is time you changed and saw things in a different light.

Additionally, when you listen, you get the chance to see a situation from the other person perspective. Many people fall into the habit of persuading others by argument. When you argue, you don't change a person's minds; instead, you make them more resistant to your efforts at persuasion.

When we talk about listening, we don't mean that you just sit and wait for the other person to stop speaking, then you start talking – no. Instead, it requires you to listen and accept the other person's position to be valid.

You Become More Knowledgeable

The truth remains that if you listen more rather than trying to find out what to do following makes you have more information to help you in your career. Listening also flatters the other person so that they give you more information than you needed. Additionally, when you demonstrate to others that you really value what they have to say, you end up appearing intelligent, and you tell them that you really appreciate what they are saying.

When you flatter someone with your attention, you make them more likely to tell you more about themselves, their priorities, and their projects. You can then use the information to persuade them more.

It Builds Relationships

When you use listening to flatter the other person, you also end up building rapport with the people who are important to the process. As an example, imagine you are in a meeting with a client and you have to persuade them that the company is the best to work with. Since you take time to demonstrate that you can listen, the client will feel that you care about their issues, and he or she will end up signing a contract with the company.

Chapter 11:
Persuasion Using Logical Reasoning, and by Leveraging One's Emotions

T here are several ways a person may be persuaded to do something. This part will deal with the two main ones: convincing people through logical reasoning and persuasion by leveraging one's emotions.

Before taking on either of these two, it is important to highlight what persuasion may achieve. In many cases, persuasion is used to elicit certain behaviors. Mostly, it is used to get people to conform to another's ideas. It may also be used t; convince people to do something they are reluctant to do, motivate people to do something they are already doing, stop them from what they are doing, or cause others to change their beliefs about something and adopt new ones. Below we will look a little deeper into these uses of persuasion while providing relevant examples. So, just what is the reason for persuasion?

To convince people to do something they are reluctant to do

It is best explained with an example. Picture a situation where you drive along a muddy road on a rainy day when your vehicle gets stuck. You try your best to maneuver the vehicle out of the mud, but it just won't budge. The road you are stuck in is not one of the main ones and is not very well-traveled by other motorists. Because of this, the chances of being towed by another truck are next to nil. Luckily, there is a diner up ahead, right around the corner. You figure out that you can get some help there, so you go. At the diner, you find a group of young men just exiting the establishment. Just what you needed, you figure.

You talk to them about your problem, and they listen. They sympathize but are reluctant to help you push your car out of the mud. They tell you that they would if they could, but they aren't willing to get dirty. The only thing left under these circumstances is to use your power of persuasion to convince them to help you. The best approach for in such a scenario is to make helping you worth their while. For instance, you may offer each a certain amount of money if they help you.

Persuasion Using Logic and Reason

Logical persuasion is the most typical form of persuasion there is. This form is so common that most people take it as the very definition of persuasion itself. Most or conversations are pegged around logic and reason. People respond better to this form of influence because they are taken through a series of compelling reasons why something should be a certain way and not the other.

If, in the end, the argument is compelling enough, the target is left with no other option but to subscribe to the new line of thought according to the reasons given. The reason behind this change is because holding onto one's beliefs or views even after being disproved beyond a reasonable doubt would make a person look stupid. Thus, persuasion using logic is favored by many. If you can make a compelling case, you can win an argument and win someone over.

Teaching

Every form of teaching at any level is an attempt at persuasion. If you take the time to consider it seriously, you will realize that all forms of education are persuasion based on logic and reason. The teacher wishes to influence his or her learners to have a particular view about something, convince them about a certain "correct" way of doing something, teach them why certain things are the way they are, or why specific actions elicit certain behaviors. To do this, teachers must rely upon logic and reason to cause their students to believe what they are saying.

Take a science lesson. Everything scientific is based on proven facts. Thus, it is not enough for the teacher to state that a specific action causes a particular reaction when teaching the subject. Instead, the teacher must go through all the logical steps that lead from an action and end in a specific reaction. While doing so, reasons must be given as to why whatever is being taught is the case. Teaching is said to be successful when a student accepts and internalizes the teacher's logical explanations. Teaching from logic and reason is the best approach since the student can apply the lessons learned elsewhere once understood. It means that logical teaching widens the student's ability as opposed to simple dictation.

Trials

Another critical area of the application of logic and reason is during trial hearings. In any trial setting, the defense and prosecution attorneys will make their cases, interrogate, cross-examine witnesses, and let the jury determine the case's verdict. Everything regarding such proceedings is pegged upon logic and reason such as when the opposing attorneys are making their opening statements. Often, to strengthen their cases, such opening statements will involve pointing out or suggesting the existence of a significant logical flaw upon which the case will be built. A defense attorney may state, for instance, that,

"By the end of this trial, the jury will determine that there is no way that the defendant could have been at the scene of the crime during the said time." Such a statement is a veiled appeal to the jury's sense of logic.

After the opening statements have been made, the attorneys go on to cross-examine their witnesses. This process relies heavily on reason and logic. For instance, when questioning their witness, a lawyer will make them appear sensible and logical. An example of a question crafted in this manner may be, "So, what did you do after finding the murder weapon? Did you contact the authorities?" Since it is the logical thing to do, the lawyer wishes to portray their witness as a straightforward and trustworthy person by employing this line of questioning.

Using logic and reason to make a witness trustworthy is double-sided. It can also be used to discredit a witness. For instance, if this was an opposing witness, the question may have been crafted as, "You mean you waited a whole hour to call the police after finding the murder weapon?" This question is bait for the opposing witness since it would be illogical to wait after finding such sensitive evidence. By questioning the witness in this manner, the attorney effectively sows doubt by poking holes in the evidence provided.

How to Use Persuasion through Logic and Reason Effectively

For persuasion to be successful, you must make a compelling case without coming on too strong and appearing coercive. Avoid unnecessary complexities when you argue your case. It is essential, especially when you reach out to a broader audience such as a classroom, a jury, or any other gathering. Simplicity means that more people will follow your argument, and in the end, you will win over more people.

If you wish to use the tactic in a conversation, beware of dominating the conversation. We risk exposing yourself to logical challenges since the more we speak, the more we give the other party ground to challenge our views. In such situations, it is advisable to speak only when necessary. Take time to listen to your opponent, weigh their words critically, and formulate your responses based it. You may be surprised that you might not need to come up with any arguments by yourself. You can gain so much ground by simply logically challenging the person based on what they say.

Given the methods of persuasion, proper preparation is essential. Winning any logical argument requires that you cover all your bases and avoid challenges. Do extensive research about any topic you wish to address beforehand. It is essential for two reasons. The first one is that research will help you gather facts to make your case more substantial and compelling. Taking time to study a particular topic will give you an upper hand against your opponent. In addition, research will make you seem well versed in a specific issue; effectively, it will provide you with authority over the issue.

Persuasion Through Emotional Leverage

Apart from using reason and logic, persuasion can be done by taking advantage of one's emotional vulnerability. It is particularly common among close people. Examples are between lovers, siblings, children, and parents or even among close friends. One can take advantage of the feelings that you have for them to persuade you into doing something.

This type of persuasion is common in family settings, for example, when children persuade their parents to buy them stuff. Before making any such requests, the child will ensure that they are first on good terms with the parent. For instance, they will be obedient to everything they are told when warming up to request. They will ensure they do everything right to endear themselves to their parents. This way, the parents will be pleased by their actions and become more inclined to consent to their requests. Notice that with this tactic, persuasion will have been achieved without any application of logic or reason. In this case, the child will have leveraged their parent's feelings for their benefit.

This persuasion tactic often works best when someone taps into feelings of sympathy from others instead of feelings of love and affection as in our example. Feigning injury, loss, or illness is a very common maneuver, especially for those who wish to get out of having to do something. For instance, your boss may not ask too many questions if you call in to say that you will not work because you feel a little under the weather. Chances are that your boss will not only grant permission for the absence but they will also wish you a quick recovery. It is a classic example of how people prey on others' emotions to persuade them to do something.

Chapter 12:
Using Body Language for Persuasion and Mind Control

K now that actions speak louder than words, so being aware of the impact that body language can have is important. With the use of non-verbal communication, you can influence the way that other people think, perceive, and act. It is a powerful concept that you have the ability to master. Being great with body language means that you not only have to use it effectively, but you also must be aware of the cues used by other people. If you are able to utilize this skill, then your positive manipulation efforts will almost always be successful.

Smile Genuinely

When you are talking to someone, simply flashing a smile can make a difference between the other person deeming you trustworthy or not. The great thing about smiling as a social cue is that it signifies many different things. It can mean you are in agreement with or understanding what the other person is saying. Without verbally saying anything in return, you can put someone at ease. This is a great tool for appearing to be accepting and inviting. This is one way you can control someone's mind by getting to the point of acceptance. Remember this during any other manipulation methods you try.

If a person is trying to humor you, smiling shows them that you find them amusing. This is a confidence booster, and it becomes especially helpful when trying to become close to someone. This action shows that you are friendly and approachable. Always share genuine smiles with other people because some are great at noticing the fake ones.

When you smile, you should mean it. Any fake action that you take will only make the other person question your intentions. Plus, you will feel better knowing that you are your true self.

The same way that smiling at others can enhance a conversation, you should also pay attention to the amount the other person smiles. Non-verbal communication is important because it says things that words sometimes can't. You will know exactly how to proceed with your positive manipulation when you know where you stand. Reading body language leaves no room for guesswork; it can be hard when you have to fill in the blanks about how someone is feeling.

Working on your smile is important if you want to appear charismatic. With this type of charisma, you become great at positive manipulation. This, combined with the ability to read other people, will provide you with a well-rounded sense of others' moods and emotions. It is normally difficult for people to hide a smile, which is why it is often a good indicator of exactly what is going on in their minds. Not only is this a great social tool, but it will also make you feel good.

Casual Touch

Touch can become a big part of social interaction once you become comfortable with it. There are definite boundaries between comfortable, casual touches and those shared only within intimate relationships. Generally, quick arm and shoulder touches are deemed appropriate when you are positively manipulating someone. Utilizing casual touch states that you understand and can relate. It makes you appear to be approachable, much like smiling can.

There are simple ways to add casual touching into your conversational skills. One of the easiest is to touch the person's arm when you are expressing words of emphasis. This will draw the other person into what you are saying. You can also incorporate touching when a deep topic is being covered.

Touching must be kept on a strictly casual basis. Remember, you want to show that you are respectful while also remaining approachable. A mistake often made is utilizing casual touching too much. Even if no boundaries are broken, it can become awkward when in excess. When you are first starting out, try only using it to place emphasis on certain things you say. There is no need to overdo it.

With any form of non-verbal communication, you can also judge a person's comfort level by how much they utilize casual touching. Arms crossed and distance being kept will normally signify that you have some more work to be done before you attempt to control the person. This closed-off body language likely means that you are not to be trusted. An open stance with some casual touching is a great sign; it means that the other person is comfortable with you. If you get these signals, you are ready to positively manipulate a situation. Sometimes, people utilize casual touching when they are nervous. If their gaze is flighty, yet casual touching is still happening, you might need to wait for a clearer signal that the person is truly comfortable with you.

Firm and Gentle Handshake

When you are in this position, you will want to remember to come across as friendly yet respectable. This balance can be tough to accomplish when you do not have an accurate handshake to match.

Put some thought into the type of message you send to other people when you first meet them. Do you have a firm grip? Do you maintain eye contact? Is there a smile on your face? All these things matter very much when it comes to your handshake.

The key to having a good handshake is having multiple different ones for different occasions. If you are in a professional setting, the handshake will naturally be firmer than a handshake you would give to a friend in a bar. The firmness of your handshake indicates the level of dominance you are trying to convey. Of course, positively manipulation does require dominant energy. You need to be the one who can change things by way of simple suggestions. If you do not maintain this role right away, you will have a lot more work to do.

Firm does not have to equal rough. You don't want to hurt the other person with your handshake. Keep the pressure at a reasonable level. Think about how you would like them to shake your own hand. There is no need to overdo the grip when you also have several other body language cues o utilize. The handshake is merely meant to provide you with a solid starting point, and then the rest can follow. When you get into the habit of shaking hands with other people, it can feel formal at first, but it is important to know how to channel your energy into getting what you want.

Eye contact plays a role in a handshake, as well. The amount of eye contact you hold can convey different messages to the other person. Not enough of it suggests that you are bluffing or weak. A person might question your motives if you appear to be distracted. Too much can be mistaken as a challenge, which you don't want. Starting conflict does not lead to positive manipulation. You should maintain enough eye contact to remain confident, but not too much that you start making others feel uncomfortable.

The Power of Correct Posture by Mirroring

You are probably familiar with the idea that you receive the energy you give. Your posture is the way you present yourself to the world. Having slumped shoulders can signify disappointment, sadness or even apathy. Keeping them pushed back with your chin up can exude confidence and pride. The way you decide to stand is very important to every single social interaction you have. Some people will follow all the correct steps of positive manipulation but forget to correct their posture. This can make all the difference.

If you are unsure about how you should present yourself to someone, simply mirror their posture. This is usually the best way to gauge your role in the given situation. If someone is being open with you, keeping their stance forward using their hands to explain things, try doing the same. When someone feels you are on the same page, it becomes much easier to converse. For those who are colder starting off, try to reel back your enthusiasm. It can be overwhelming when one person is clearly expressing that it will take some time to become comfortable, and the other person continues to push boundaries. Your best bet is to remain as neutral as you can until the other person does something to indicate otherwise.

When you mirror a person's posture, don't make it obvious. Of course, you do not want to copy their exact mannerisms. This becomes insulting or comical. You can still be on the same page without doing the exact same thing. If your boss is angry, your endless banter and casual touching won't make the best impression. Each situation will be different, so you must use common sense. It is best to accept anger and disappointment exactly as they are presented. Keep a strong physical stance but remain facing the person. By turning away, it suggests that you are closed off or do not care about what is being explained.

When someone is ready to express happiness, they will stand a lot closer to you. They might even smile a lot and partake in casual touching. When you experience this, you know that you can also relax a bit more during the interaction. As you match the behaviors, the demeanor also becomes synchronized. It is impossible to do this with someone who cannot empathize. It takes a truly empathetic person to be able to mirror any type of posture, good or bad.

Eye Contact

Eye contact is an extremely relevant form of non-verbal communication. The eyes hold plenty of valuable information behind them. A simple furrow of the brow can reveal true feelings in an instant. It is thought that maintaining eye contact with someone makes you a more trustworthy person. Being able to look into someone's eyes without wavering suggests you are being genuine. For whatever reason, eye contact can be hard for a lot of people. Even if you value your honesty and integrity, maintaining eye contact with someone during a conversation can take some practice.

We tend to shy away from eye contact because it has the ability to make us feel vulnerable. While you do not need to completely drop your guard around those you make eye contact with, you do need to make sure that you are trusting them to the best of your own ability. This mutual reciprocation will give you the certainty that you can make a positive influence in this person's life. It shows that the interaction goes beyond any surface-level small talk that normally occurs. Just as giving eye contact can be hard, it might also be hard to interact with someone who gives it too intensely.

It is best to not engage in such challenging behaviors. Remember, you must be in control of how the situation flows. Keep things as positive as you can but know that you should ultimately be the one who is guiding how everything unfolds. You will want to place yourself in a position of power without the other person fully realizing it. This is what gives you the upper hand with positive manipulation. Be aware of the eye contact you do maintain in your daily life and think about ways to improve it. Do you need to do it more often? Could you do without some of it? Are you making people feel the way you need them to feel? All of these questions must be taken into consideration.

You will find that eye contact is one of the most powerful forms of body language that exists. It can hold so much expression behind it because of the way our eyes seem to tell silent stories. When a person is experiencing pain or hardship, you will likely see it in their gaze before they express it to you. These are things that you need to look out for. You should always aim to be one step ahead of what the other person is thinking or feeling, coming up with valuable solutions that can be implemented.

Chapter 13:
Influencing People with N.L.P.

W ords are powerful, or should we say that words are power. The meanings of them crystallize our perceptions and shape our vision and beliefs. In turn, words create our world. How are they so powerful? Because we make them so since we give them the power to create everything around us and give meaning to everything we know. Say the word "fire" in the workplace, and you can see the powerful emotional and energetic reactions of the people there.

Words are the essential and powerful tools you have. Until now, whatever you have learned from this guide was based upon words, how to effectively use them, how to find out which words impact the most, and how to make sure that your words form an impact, etc. Now, we will see the power of words on their own and the different influencing techniques used in N.L.P. that could not be categorized otherwise.

The Power of Words

Let's dive into some real science to understand the power of words. Words can change our genes. Positive words like peace or love can alter genes' expressions, strengthen our frontal lobe areas, and promote our brain's cognitive functions. They propel the motivational centers of our minds and, in short, have the power to impact us vastly.

To understand how this works, we have to learn how our brain derives meaning from the world around us. We see an image, and of all the bits of information, we select a specific amount to be processed by our brains. This specific information chosen is based on our profiles. After we have this information, we start to assign meaning to it. We give meaning by comparing new information to our past experiences and knowledge; and once the meaning is derived, the real game starts, but you have no clue what is going on inside your head. Once the meaning is derived and concluded, our brains start to release certain chemicals hormones, or neurotransmitters so you can feel the moment and react accordingly.

Let me give you an example. Imagine you see a dog running towards you from a distance. This scene in your mind is compared to past experiences with dogs (that, let's say, are wrong), and your brain releases chemicals of fear and hate. Your brains assign these negative words to the scene, "dangerous" or "lethal," and, thus, you react accordingly.

We can see here how words play significant roles in our deep psychology, and thus how we use them is very important. If we develop the ability to analyze scenes and assign meanings to them ourselves, we can control our lives. On the other hand, we can persuade other people more effectively and efficiently with the use of words.

Interrogations

Many techniques are used by policemen and investigators based on words alone, and they show remarkable efficiency. One such method is making the accused say, "yes" many times. How does this work? Well, once we say something over and over again, we feel more comfortable saying it. Thus, if you ask a liar a lot of questions that lead to the simple answer of "yes", then ask them about the thing they have done, as they might say yes.

It is not 100% effective, but it works. Another method is by making someone confess to lower crimes first. Ask the accused whether they have ever smoked a cigarette, and if they have, they won't hesitate to say yes to that; but this answer will make them more accustomed to confessing (because most people think of smoking as a taboo). Then ask them if they have ever stolen something in their childhood, how many lies they tell in a day, and to think about other guilty things they might have committed. Once you have established these questions, then ask about the real crime. There is a high possibility they are merely going to confess.

Truism

A truism is a cliché statement that is highly effective when trying to manipulate someone or playing the game of words. Such information, if used correctly, may give a reliable back-up to your statement. The truism method of manipulation is straightforward and is not something related to real truism.

For example, say you are debating with someone online about a particular world-history topic. What you do is give nine real facts or figures, with sources and references, and the 10th one you give is without any source of citation. In fact, it is a lie. People are just going to believe you. That's how people are.

You can build the trust of someone by merely telling them true things a couple of times, and in the meantime, you can feed them some lies, and they are just going to believe them.

When you want to use truism, there are two ways to start. Either do your homework on the person you want to feed lies to. It would make a great start because you can feed them the truths or facts you have researched to gain their trust. On the contrary, if you have a vast knowledge of many fields, or the fields humans tend to know about, then you don't have to do much homework.

Let's take an example. There is a girl in your class who is a somewhat religious conservative type. Now, you want her not to be so because you feel bad for her. If you go and talk to her directly, there is absolutely no way she will let you question her core beliefs. But you can make her question herself.

Start with random talk, totally kind and comfortable. Help her with her homework and the like. Step one is done. Now do some research on her religion and get the loopholes. If you are using logic, there are always loopholes in every possible thing. Even if the scripture is well written and you don't want to reject the entire religion, you omit where the scripture tells people to be social and meet and greet. Then you can exaggerate it and add a few clauses of your own. Your perfect lie is made. Now you have to implant it in her head.

You tell many things about her religion in your talks because now you have done your research. You talk about the history and the obvious things so she trusts you as a credible source. Once you think it is time, you randomly tell her about your perfect lie. Trust me, she is going to buy it in no time. She won't be able to say no because you never lied about any other points, and she starts to question her own beliefs.

You ignited an internal fight and leave her to it, or you can help her along the way. Now let us combine some other things we have learned so far. You mirror and match her and keep her in perfect rapport all the time you spend with her, even if it's barely 5 minutes. It creates an exception for you in her mind, and she would trust not only your words but also you in person. After she is done with her internal fight, be there for her, tell her more about the religion and various other things, while reporting and feeding her lies that lead her to your own life philosophy. The game is simple. Now she will start to admire and trust you; she has an image of you in mind because she became a better version of herself. She could even fall in love with you.

Hidden Commands

You would be astonished to see that other than the general methods of manipulation and persuasion, there are also some specific phrases and commands to persuade people. Salespeople use them the most.

Weasel Phrases

Tell people how good they'll feel by buying your product or agreeing to your plan. "Imagine how good you'll feel."

Tag Questions

Questions that have "isn't" it, aren't they, etc., are hard to disagree with, and extremely hard for some people.

Perhaps not Quite

Tell them you will not advise them to buy your product until they are delighted and have done their research.

Relax

Tell them to relax.

Other Words

You can use any word in the English language that most people are familiar and associated with a certain feeling as a command phrase or word.

That said, now, if you look at the method, you will be able to understand its implications and use it effectively.

Chapter 14:
Using Social Pressure in Persuasion

N ow that you have scaled the possible heights of persuasion operating at its most substantial level, consider that it will take you years to get to that point. Yet you may very well need the ability to persuade now. Your starting place does affect the road you should take through the land of persuasion. This chapter is about using social pressure for positive persuasion.

Peer Pressure

As a result of popular culture, peer pressure is often viewed as an absolute negative and minor moral wrong. You may remember, depending upon your upbringing, one of the classic clichés of situational comedy television shows.

For example, a mother picks her child up from school to find that he has been in detention for doing something wrong. Say for this exercise that he was caught trying to leave school with a group of friends instead of going to class. The mother, fed up with her son, asks him why he did what he did. In response, her son says something along the lines of, "Everybody else was cutting class!" or "Everybody else was doing it!" Exasperated, his mother snaps back at him, "So if everybody was jumping off a cliff, would you do that, too?" Depending on the show's silliness, the son may reply, "How high?" or something else implying he would consider it.

It is an excellent example of the cultural understanding of how peer pressure functions. Firstly, it is shown to be an apparent negative force. It is indicated by a poor decision on the part of the boy and why his mother is so angry with him. Secondly, it is shown to be a childish force, something that people grow out of with time. You can tell this plainly from the fact that his mother is above peer pressure and from the fact that it is a school-aged boy shown as being susceptible to it.

What is more, it is shown to be simultaneously one of the failings of youth. The joke at the end implies that despite its lightness in tone, the boy is so inclined to follow the herd he would risk injury to do it. This cliché is an interesting case study in that it can show what culture and the media at large get wrong about peer pressure.

In reality, peer pressure is none of the things indicated from the cliché just elaborated upon in the preceding paragraph. For one, peer pressure is not an inalienable force in the minds of those under its sway. In point of fact, like all other external drivers of behavior, it can and should be checked regularly by a person's own internal moral, ethical, and otherwise responsible compass. Additionally, peer pressure is not dependent on age to nearly the same degree as the cliché implies.

While it seems correct to children because they are learning all the time and always testing boundaries and experimenting with different behavior, they may occasionally have skewed perspectives on when it is appropriate or inappropriate to follow the herd. Adults are more than susceptible to peer pressure as well. In a certain sense, peer pressure is just a kind of conformity. Everyone loves to conform, and very often following along with the herd and capitulating to the pressures of peers is a means to do just that. Most importantly, the third portion this cliché gets it wrong as peer pressure is not an inherently negative thing.

Persuasion comes in in spades and peer pressure is always already a rudimentary form of it. It is true and self-evident because one's peers pressuring one to do something is a one-to-one comparison, which is to say completely congruous, with one's peers persuading one to do something. Having made it this far in the book, you understand that persuasion gets an unearned bad rap in quite a bit of our culture, so is it any surprise that this elemental and natural form of persuasion is lambasted in television comedies? It should come as a surprise. However, more to the point is the fact that like all forms of persuasion, peer pressure can be leveraged for a complete degree of positive changes in a person's life.

Peer pressure with the right peers can be a source of inspiration to achieve better things and be your best self.

Guiding the Pack to Guide Individual Behavior

However, a question that may arise is how one might go about utilizing peer pressure when it is such a nebulous thing and out of necessity driven by a group and not an individual. The answer to this is simple; you must lead the group as a whole.

The concept of the indirect leader, for instance, has a long and storied history. An indirect leader chooses to avoid the spotlight and even neglects or outright rejects, taking on an official role as a leader. It is the ideal method of wielding leadership and power for someone interested in persuasion to begin with. Still, if you are shy about taking command socially, it has the added benefit of not marking you as a leader in group settings.

So, how would it work? Imagine, in answer to that a group of children who are all friends with each other and semi-regularly spend time playing altogether. When they are not playing as a whole, they play in loose groups comprised of some number of members, and these loose groups change such that every child spends time with every other child in between each meeting of the whole group. If one of these children were interested in guiding this group's behavior, they would need only to work to their influence slowly. By way of the rudimentary techniques or by some other machination - if he or she is so inclined - of individual members of each subgroup of children. By this metric, the wise child would be able to, slowly but surely, affect the behavior of the entire group.

Chapter 15:
Persuasion in Sales and Marketing

P ersuasion is an essential aspect of any business. It is, in fact, the basis of any business. Therefore, anyone who wants to go into a business online or generally should learn all the rudiments of communicative persuasion.

Persuasion, as a concept, is evident in every form of communication. That is why it was stated earlier that everyone at some point in their lives must have used persuasion. For effective business communication, persuasion is needed. Without correctly understanding how to use persuasion, the business owner might fall short of new customers and find it hard to win people over to their ideas. Here's a list of those who might need to use persuasion:

- The owner of a small or big business trying to get a customer
- A person or a company trying to get a contract
- A staff member with a sales pitch
- An employee
- A company who is into media and wants to advertise a product to specific people
- Finally, a customer

During any bargain, the customer also tries to convince the seller that the price should be brought down to both parties' convenience. The question now is how to persuade a person to agree with a person in business?

Understand Your Audience

The audience is not necessarily broad; it could also be a single person or a small group. One of the essential parts of any communication is knowing and understanding the audience. This same criticality is also evident in most business persuasion. Those who own a business must be very wary of passing information whether to an individual or a group of individuals. You have to know what they expect, what they want, and what the outcome will be of what is intended. In a nutshell, you need to know what their objective is for business.

An example is when an employee who wants to go to a conference and is looking to take permission from a boss might only be interested in the budget issue. The employee can make the boss see why information from that conference will be beneficial for the meeting. First, the employee will have to analyze the boss' interest in helping the employee better his communication with the right persuasive messages.

Another example is when a businessman is looking to sell a product. You should know exactly why your customer will likely to buy your product and how it will benefit them. By making these findings, the approach will be more comfortable, which brings us to the next step.

Choosing the Right Medium

After knowing your audience and seeing their interest, it is now essential to analyze what medium of communication they would prefer. Trying to tell a boss about your absence from work over the phone is not a good idea. People want to get messages differently, and some customers are prone to being convinced to get things in different ways. It is accurate because it is the wrong medium of communication based on the situation.

An example is when you want to stop to meet with a colleague unexpectedly to discuss a very vital issue. It is only agreeable if the colleague is okay with it. If not, an email should be first put forward or preferably a call based on what the other colleague wants. In essence, for proper persuasive communication, it is vital to use a medium that is very appropriate for both to the message being passed and per audience's preference.

Taking Time to Listen

Passing information is not a one-way thing. When communicating to yourself, you are only telling yourself what it is you already know. When trying to persuade another party, one should pay close attention to what the person is saying. This way, you will understand that a person's emotional state and the power to use it to get what you want.

In most types of communication, it is usually two-way, which is the most effective way to persuade an audience. Often, communicators are so focused on what they want that they fail to understand the point of view or the audience's emotional state. They do not take time to listen. As much as trying to speak is essential in persuasion, listening is also necessary. It can help one understand the audience's desires, motivations, interests, and concerns. We have tried to explain that as much as you would like to reach your communication goal, it is also essential to sit back and listen to your audience.

Building a Strong Relationship

Having good communication is essential in a healthy relationship. You cannot persuade a boss without having a good relationship with the person.

You cannot persuade an audience or customer without first building a good relationship. It is on the foundation of a good relationship that both the business owner and the customer or a colleague can communicate better. Through strong relationships, regularity is ensured in business. We can share even our most sensitive issues with whoever we have built a stable and healthy relationship. We can pass on the information and get feedback. Taking time to groom and develop connections even before trying to persuade will make a significant difference in your success.

An example is when an employee is trying to persuade a boss but has always come late to work or in submitting jobs. It's easy to predict that the boss will likely not accept the proposal. The employee has not left a good impression or built a good reputation with the boss.

When one wants to persuade, persuasion is a tool used to get new clients, a good worker, and generally move the business to a better level. People who know how to persuade are influential, and people like these types. They are usually the quiet ones in the room. They speak less, but they eventually do. They make sense and can make people do things. They also make sure to put the needs of others above their own. Here are the habits of an excellent persuasive businesspersons:

Curiosity and Listening

As stated in how to persuade people in a business, one should have the habit of listening to effectively persuade another. You would need to know what others want on both an emotional and a physical level. You should make sure to ask the right questions and again listen when the person is speaking. You should be open-ended when beginning discussions. You should demonstrate a genuine interest in what others do. If you can understand by listening, persuasion will come quickly. When you want to know and be attentive, you have automatically sent a message that you value the person. With time, your reputation of trustworthiness will grow.

Honesty

Honesty is usually a quality required in any business to be successful. In essence, for a business to thrive, it has to have a benchmark on transparency. It also goes for anyone who is looking to persuade in business. Your credibility and ability to persuade depend on your ability to be very honest in all situations. Dishonesty is very destructive and capable of misleading others. An intentional lie can ruin your professional reputation. Indeed, the truth might sometimes hurt, but it is better to be honest than to lose trust due to dishonesty.

Confidence

Be it a customer, client, or colleague, you should learn to be confident. The place of confidence cannot be side-lined in business. You should know how to show that you believe in your ideas and your proposal. Be confident in what you are selling. Being confident when showing a product will convince a potential customer that what you have to offer is genuinely useful. To avoid anxiety or even self-doubt, remain calm when presenting anything. Straightforwardness should be used, and do not dabble about the whole thing. State your position and validate it with clear facts.

Effective Voicing

Once you have said something, people will begin to make decisions based on how you have communicated with them. When communicating, it is advisable to speak slowly and know when to raise your voice to speak loudly but still clearly. Making use of brief pauses will make being clear easier. Emphasize your points better and avoid fillers like "uh".

Tell a Story

People will enjoy your speech better when you chip in a story. A well-told story is enjoyable and themed towards what you have to offer. Stories can persuade others in the business. It is always good to move away from the stress of business in telling a good story. As opposed to facts, the way people pay attention differs. Your story must connect with what the client is thinking, what they believes, and what you intend them to believe.

Chapter 16:
How to Win Friends

Be Friendly

To influence and persuade other people to fall within your circle of friends, you must be friendly. A friendly disposition is a fundamental requirement that makes someone quite attractive to other people, thus resulting in long-lasting relationships. Your body language is perhaps one of the most central aspects that enables you to cultivate a friendly disposition.

For instance, learning to smile once every so often whenever interacting with other people is considered a vital aspect of effective body language. Furthermore, leaning forward and maintaining eye contact during conversations is also an appropriate body language that tells other people that you are indeed an approachable person who can quickly get along with other people. All in all, being friendly to other people through the use of appropriate body language will ensure that you are able to influence their perception of what they think about you, thus enhancing your ability to make friends.

Advise but Do Not Criticize

Many people do not take kindly to criticism. More often than not, people want to be made to feel that their position on any issue is the correct one, but this is not always the case. Persuasion and influence are essential when you want to correct other people or offer an alternative perspective.

Avoid criticizing at any cost and, instead, offer your advice as an alternative way of looking at an issue. In the same breath, it is equally important to point out that you agree with the perspective of others before outlining areas you think might need further improvements. This approach enabled you to put across your views without necessarily having to criticize the opinions expressed by those around you.

Be a Good Role Model

The saying, birds of a feather flock together, applies very well when it comes to friendships. This simply means that people usually tend to identify with other people with whom they share common values and principles. Being a good role model enables one to cultivate the right values that will allow them to attract many friends. For instance, values such as honesty, hard work, and commitment are considered universally attractive and go a long way in making one a good role model in society.

Espousing such values, therefore, makes one attractive to other people who also cherish them as a role model. For instance, it is quite common to find that the circle of friends of a successful CEO is comprised of equally high accomplishing individuals. All of them value hard work and commitment such that these values are the glue that holds them together. Being a good role model affords one an opportunity to define who they are and attract like-minded individuals into their circle of friends.

Make Other People Feel Important

In order to influence, persuade, and win over other people, you must make them feel that they matter. Another person can only identify themselves as your friend if they are made to feel that they matter to you. This is very important, especially when it comes to relationships between individuals who might not be at the same status or stage in life. For instance, the CEO of a high-profile company can only establish a friendship relationship with low cadre employees such as the janitors if the former actually go out of their way to instill some level of self-confidence and high self-esteem in them. In this example, the CEO can schedule periodic meetings with all categories of employees, including the very junior ones. They can freely interact and exchange ideas on issues affecting the company. By doing this, the CEO will make the janitors and other low-level employees feel equally important within the organizational setting. The CEO will thus be in a better position to establish a long-lasting friendship with their employees, consequently, creating the kind of synergy that will enhance overall organizational performance.

How to Interest People

Being able to draw the attention and interest of other people is a valuable tip when it comes to winning friends. People must be able to identify with you before they can commit to being your friend. It is therefore vital that you are in a position to take various steps to make them realize who you are, what you stand for, and make them understand that your ideas actually resonate with theirs. To sell your ideas to others, you have to capture their interest and make them understand that whatever it is you are proposing is something that will actually add value to their lives.

Identify with Their Issues

Most people will be interested in what you have to say or your opinion on something if you are talking about an issue they identify with.

Different people are faced with various problems, and it is vital to understand some of their issues to interest these other people. This is despite the fact that you might not be experiencing some of the problems in question. For instance, you might come from a wealthy background and thus are not facing any socio-economic issues.

However, someone you wish to befriend might be coming from a poor background and is faced with a myriad of socio-economic challenges. In such a scenario, the most effective way to earn their interest is to identify with some of the challenges they are facing even if your circumstances are different. This might entail letting them know that you know what they are going through and are willing to offer them any assistance needed.

Sometimes, such assistance might not even be in the form of material support. This is because some of the issues that other people are experiencing might not necessarily relate to material things but have more to do with their emotional state. For instance, someone might be experiencing an emotional breakdown or even depression. Like a good friend or a potential one, all you need to do is offer them advice and the necessary assurance that all will be fine.

Be a Good Listener

Listening is one of the more vital soft skills that can help enhance interpersonal relationships, but it is often ignored. The best way to learn more about other people is by listening. You will be able to identify the challenges they might be facing, their goals and objectives in life, and their fears, hobbies and additional vital information that will improve your capacity to interact and form mutually beneficial relationships.

A true friend is one who actually takes the time to know the other person and strives to be a better friend each and every other day. For example, if you know some of the goals and objectives of another person, you will be in a better position to assist them in the attainment of the same. In turn, the other person will appreciate you much more and consider you to be their true friend. Furthermore, by having an understanding of another person's fears and challenges, you will be able to avert situations that might activate such fears.

Know People by Their Names

People usually find it more compelling when you refer to them by their names, especially during an initial interaction. Many people assume that you do not know them by names, but once you refer to them by their names, they become surprised and are more than willing to indulge you. Furthermore, it is very annoying when someone within your social setting knows you by your name but somehow, you cannot seem to remember theirs. For instance, a colleague at work might refer to you by name and put you in an awkward position as far as the interaction is concerned since you cannot seem to remember theirs. In such a situation, the other person might dismiss you as an arrogant or a self-centered individual who does not pay significant attention to other people.

You might probably never be able to win their interest if this is the case. Therefore, knowing other people's names and referring to them during initial interactions can be the start of a long-lasting friendship. They will feel appreciated since someone actually took the time to know their names and, in turn, they will appreciate you for it. They will be more likely to listen keenly to what you have to say, respond positively to any reasonable request, and even be willing to accept future engagements such as a date, meeting or night out.

Share a Personal Story

Friendship is mainly all about trust. This implies that two people who call each other friends should be able to trust one another, sometimes with their deepest secrets. Many people might fear to do so since it might make them vulnerable to other people.

However, if done the right way, it should enable you to win the interest and trust of the other person. A correct approach would, for instance, allow other people a peep into your personal life by telling something close to you that could be used by a malicious person to undermine your reputation. This might be something as mundane as personal phobias not have formerly shared with anyone else. By sharing such information, the other person will definitely take much more interest in you; but at the same time, trust you with their personal stories.

Chapter 17:
Mirroring and Persuasion

M irroring is another nonverbal influence that is useful in the art of persuasion. Mirroring is the act of imitating the body language, attitude, and speech pattern of another person. Most of the time when mirroring occurs, it is an unconscious act because most people want to fit in; and thus, they mirror the actions of the person who seems the most authoritative. Kids are the most prolific example as they copy the actions of their parents, other adults, friends, and their peers. They even mirror their favorite fictional characters! We have all seen little boys take on the stance of and repeat the most loved superhero's words.

Adults mirror, too, even though it is not as obvious to spot sometimes. Mirroring is an evolutionary instinct passed down from the time the first human beings walked the earth. We do this by assessing other people when we first meet them. This assessment determines whether or not the people in that environment will positively or negatively impact us. The determination is made by seeing if they mirror us.

Mirroring can, off the bat, seem rather creepy if you are not familiar with the concept or do not understand its psychology. Therefore, let's get rid of that factor by explaining the necessity of the act.

Mirroring is a bonding experience that allows us to be accepted by groups such as our family and friends and is a way to build rapport with new people. We usually do this without realizing we are doing it. The unconscious factor is a leftover survival instinct that came from the evolution of the human species. It was because of mirroring that we were able to leave small caveman societies behind to form the human civilizations we now have. In its most basic form, mirroring is a nonverbal way of saying, "Look at me. We are the same. Therefore, we can co-exist compatibly."

The urge to mirror is seen in a few common examples such as the contagion of yawning. When one person yawns, it usually sets off everyone in the room to do the same even if the other person only heard the yawn. Another example is how we form lines naturally in settings like a bank or restaurant without being told to do so. Many people have found themselves waiting in the wrong line because their body followed the urge to mirror without their mind questioning if this was the right action to mirror.

You might be wondering who we naturally mirror in a group setting. The answer is that most people naturally mirror the most authoritative figure or the leader in a group setting. Most employees in a company will mirror the typical company gestures and attitudes rather than anyone else's. Even if no one says who the leader in a group setting is, it is easy to guess based on body language. That person usually displays the most dominant body language, such as standing tall or sitting at the head of a table. The others in that setting follow that lead and display more submissive body language. It is also apparent how other people will naturally adopt that person's body language.

The effect of mirroring is by gender. Women tend to mirror other women more naturally compared to men mirroring other men. Women also tend to mirror men without issue, while men are a lot less likely to mirror women unless men are engaged in courtship. This natural inclination for mirroring by women is possible because most women are more naturally intuitive and in tune with their emotions. Women are better able to pick up and decipher body language and nonverbal cues and thus are keener to mirror.

Even though women are more naturally inclined to natural mirroring, anyone can learn to use the technique. As with any learned skill, most people do not get it right at first, but practice makes perfect, or at least something close. The following guide offers a golden process for using mirroring in the art persuasion.

How to Mirror Successfully

When mirroring is done effectively, it is a powerful tool in the art of persuasion. It allows the person being persuaded to feel more connected with the persuader and makes the persuader's job easier only if the person being persuaded thinks the connection is genuine. Therefore, you need to use mirroring to persuade someone else to build that connection. Here is what you need to do:

- Give this person your full attention by facing them squarely. It is known as fronting.
- Keep adequate eye contact. Remember that eye contact can be a funny thing. Too much or too little can ruin the act of building that connection.
- Nod when this person is speaking. It serves several purposes. It makes the person speak for longer and, thus, gives you more clues about what you can say or do to persuade them. Nodding also implies that you agree with this person, which builds rapport and makes the person feel more inclined to agree with you.

These actions should make this person feel like they are the center of your universe. People love having attention focused on them even if they do not realize it.

Once that connection has been formed, work on mimicking speech patterns. It amplifies the connection that has been developed. Most people make the mistake when using the mirroring technique in persuasion because they focus on mirroring physical actions – a dead giveaway that they are copying this person - rather than nonverbal cues. The easiest way to mirror someone else subtly is to copy the pace and volume of their speech. For example, if this person is soft spoken and level-toned with their tone's inflection, adopt the same pattern of speech. If, instead, this person is animated and loud in inflection, the same applies. Adopt that pattern of speech instead.

After you have successfully mirrored the pace and volume of this person's speech pattern, you try to mirror posture and gestures. The next step in a successful mirror is to identify then use the punctuator the person being persuaded uses. A punctuator is a gesture that someone uses to emphasize or make their point clear. Just like punctuation makes the meaning of written communication so much clearer for people to understand, so do nonverbal punctuators. Most people use their hands to add a nonverbal emphasis to their words. Facial expressions like a raised eyebrow or a tilt of the lips are also commonly observed.

As the persuader, it is your job to note what this punctuator is and then to use it to show commonality between you and this person. Let's illustrate how this works with a story:

A woman is trying to get into her boss's good graces so that she can eventually broach the subject of getting a promotion for a post that will be available soon. It is a small company, and the culture is laid back, so it is not uncommon for the boss to joke and be more casual. The persuader, hoping to land that post, is having lunch with the boss, and the two women are discussing an issue that gets the boss excited. She notices that the woman flicks her fingers when she becomes this animated.

She nodded and fronted as she listened to the woman's speech about her take, and when the boss finished this speech, she used the same flicking gesture that the boss had used. The boss's face light's up, and she says, "Right!" as the staff member had just agreed with her even though the woman had not said a word. It immediately makes the staff member more memorable and favored in the boss's eyes.

After finding and using this punctuator, it is time to test the connection you have developed. The point is to note if this person will mirror you back. While you do not have to do this last step, it allows you to gauge how easily the person will adopt your action and, thus, your way of thinking. For example, you may decide to stretch your fingers, which has not been done during the current bout of conversation, to see if this person does the same.

Once you have established this connection, you can bring forth your case of persuasion. Remember to keep things as subtle as possible so that the person does not go on the defensive.

The Don'ts of Mirroring

While it is great to have a process for successful mirroring, all that work will be wasted if you slip up. It is essential to know what to do, and it is also equally important to know what not to do. Here are a few tips of what you should not do when it comes to mirroring:

- Do not try to be interested in what this person is saying if you are genuinely not as this person will mostly realize your interest is not authentic. It will hurt your case more than it will help it. It also damages your relationship with this person.
- Do not try to mirror the other person's accent or any unusual phrases used by this person. You run the risk that the person will think you are ridiculing them.
- Never use negative nonverbal cues to mirror such as a closed body posture like crossed arms and looking away. It breaks the connection you have built. Always use positive nonverbal cues instead.
- Don't mirror the other person's body language, gestures, and facial expressions precisely, as this will seem suspicious and put the person's guard up.
- Do not test the connection more than once.
- Do not focus too hard on mirroring another person that it stresses you out, as this will likely show in your body language, gestures, and facial expression, and cause the opposite reaction.

Chapter 18:
Dark Persuasion Techniques

A fter taking a look at the different types of persuasion and what they all mean, you may now see why dark persuasion is such a bad thing and can be harmful to the victim. Being able to recognize the different techniques that the manipulator uses can make it easier to understand when it is being used on you.

So, how exactly is a dark persuader able to use his or her wiles to carry out their wishes? There are a few different tactics that a dark manipulator is going to use, but some of the most common are:

The Long Con

The first method is the Long Con. It is kind of slow and drawn out, but it can be really effective because it takes so long and is hard to recognize when something goes wrong. Some of the main reasons why some people have the ability to resist persuasion are because they feel they are being pressured by the other person, and this can make them back off. If they feel there is a lack of rapport or trust with the person trying to persuade them, they will steer clear. The Long Con is so effective because the victim is able to overcome these main problems and gives the persuader exactly what they want.

The Long Con of the dark persuader takes time to earn the trust of the victim. They befriend the victim and make sure that he or she trusts and likes them. This is achieved by artificial rapport building, which sometimes seems excessive, and other techniques help to increase the comfort level between the persuader and the victim.

As soon as the persuader sees that the victim is properly readied psychologically, the persuader begins their attempt. They may start out with some insincere positive persuasion by leading their victim into making a choice or doing some action that will actually benefit the persuader. This serves the persuader in two ways. First, the victim starts to become used to the persuasion. The second is that the victim is going to start making a mental association between a positive outcome and the persuasion. The Long Con takes a long period of time to implement because the persuader doesn't want to make it too obvious what they are doing.

Graduality

Often when we hear about acts of dark persuasion, it seems impossible and unbelievable. Dark persuasion is more like a staircase. The dark persuader is never going to ask the victim to do something big and dramatic the first time they meet; instead, they will have the victim take one step at a time.

When the manipulator has the target go one step at a time, the whole process seems less of a big deal. Before the victim knows it, they have already gone a long way down, and the persuader isn't likely to let them come back up again.

Let's take an example of how this process looks in real life. Let's say that there is a criminal who wants to make it look like someone else committed their crimes. Gang bosses, cult leaders, and even Charles Manson have done this exact same thing.

The criminal wouldn't dream of asking their victim to murder for them. This would send out a red flag, and no one in their right mind would willingly go out and kill for someone they barely knew. Instead, the criminal would start out by having the victim do something small like a petty crime or simply hiding a weapon.

Over time, the acts the manipulator is able to persuade their victim to do become more severe. And since they did the smaller crimes, the persuader now has the unseen leverage of holding some of those smaller misdeeds over the victim's head, kind of like for blackmail. Before the victim knows it, they are going to feel that they are in too deep. They will then be persuaded to carry out some of the most shocking crimes. By this point, they will do it because they feel they have no other choice.

Dark persuaders are experts at using graduality to increase the severity of their persuasion over time. They know that no victim would be willing to jump over the canyon and do the big crime or misdeed right away. So, the persuader works to build a bridge to get there. By the time the victim sees how far in they are, it is too late to turn back.

Masking the True Intentions

There are different methods that a persuader uses in dark psychology to get the things they want. Disguising their true desires is very important to be successful. The best persuaders use this approach in a variety of ways, but the method they choose often depends on the victim and the situation.

One principle used by a persuader is where many people have a difficult time refusing two requests when they happen in a row. Let's say that the persuader wants to get $200 from the victim, but they do not intend to repay the money. To start, the persuader may begin by saying that they need a loan for $1000. They may go into some detail about the consequences to themselves if the persuader doesn't come up with the money sometime soon.

It may happen that the victim feels some kind of guilt or compassion toward the persuader, and they want to help. But $1000 is a lot of money, and more than the victim is able to lend. From here, the persuader lessens their request from $1000 down to $200, the amount they wanted from the beginning. Of course, there is some emotional reason for needing the money, and the victim feels like it is impossible to refuse this second request. They want to help out the persuader, and they feel bad for not giving in to the initial request. In the end, the persuader gets the $200, and the victim is not going to know what had taken place.

Another technique is known as reverse psychology. This masks the true intentions of the persuasion. Some people have a personality known as a boomerang. They will refuse to go in the direction they are thrown and instead will veer off into a different one.

If the persuader knows someone who is a boomerang type, then they are able to identify a key weakness of that person. For example, a persuader has a friend who is attempting to win over a girl they like. The persuader knows that the friend will use and then hurt that girl. The girl is currently torn between a malicious friend and an innocent third party. The persuader may try to steer the girl in the direction of the guy who is actually a good choice, knowing that she is going to go against this and end up with the harmful friend.

Leading Questions

Another method of dark persuasion is known as leading questions. Leading questions are any questions intended to trigger a specific response from the victim. The persuader may ask the target something like "How bad do you think those people are?" This question implies that the people the persuader is asking about are definitely bad to some extent. They could have chosen to ask a question that was non-leading such as, "How do you feel about those people?"

Dark persuaders are masters at using leading questions in a way that is hard to catch. If the victim ever begins to feel they are being led, then they are going to resist, and it will be hard to lead or persuade them. If a persuader ever senses that their victim starts to catch on to what is happening, they will quit using that one question and switch over to another. They may come back to the first tactic, but only when the victim has quieted down a bit and is more influenceable.

The Law of State Transference

This is a tactic that takes a look at the general mood someone is in. If someone is aligned with their deeds, words, and thoughts, this is an example of a strong and congruent state. The law involves the concept of someone who holds the balance of power in a situation who can then transfer their emotional state onto the other person they are interacting with.

Initially, the influencer is going to force their own state to match the state of their target. If the target is sad and they talk slowly, the influencer is going to make their own state follow this format. The point is to create a deep rapport with the target. After we get to this state match, the influencer alters their own state subtly to see if they have some compliance for the victim. Perhaps, they will choose to speed up their own voice to see if the victim will speed up as well.

Once the victim starts to show signs of compliance, this is an indication that the influencer is at the hook point.

As soon as this hook point is reached, though it may take some time depending upon the target and the situation, the influencer is going to change their own personal state to the one they want the victim to have.

This could be an emotional state. It could be positive, angry, happy, or indignant. It often depends on what the persuader wants to help reach their goals. This technique is an important one for a dark persuader because it is going to show the impact of subconscious cues on the failure or success of any type of persuasion.

Chapter 19:
Self-Persuasion

Self-persuasion is one of the most powerful and most challenging areas of persuasion. Where the other forms of persuasion are applied from an external force, self-persuasion comes from within. So how can persuasion be used as a technique?

First, self-persuasion can use as a method to persuade others indirectly. For effectiveness, self-persuasion must come from within. In other words, a person decides without being told what to think directly. Persuading someone using self-persuasion involves setting up a situation where the other person comes to the desired conclusion because of what they have learned. Given what they know, they can come to no different conclusion.

Self-persuasion is a useful technique to employ in association with some reward. If a person behaves in a certain way and receives a benefit, afterwards, they will conclude that it must be right. We'll look at the techniques of self-persuasion on others more at the end of this guide. Let's look first the most beneficial methods self-persuasion as a means of personal development.

Personal Development

Persuasion techniques don't work well when we try to use them on ourselves because we realize what we're doing. It's like trying to use persuasion tactics on another person overtly. If they know we're trying to persuade them, they tend to fight against what we're asking them to do.

Our minds are the same way. So how do we end up doing things we don't want to do over and over again? One way is that we accidentally create habits that aren't beneficial. Because these tend to be associated with a reward, we do them repeatedly until the practice is developed. For instance, we eat candy because it tastes so good, but we create a habit of taking in many calories that aren't good for us. We eventually figure this out and try to make changes, but our old ways are too easy to fall back on. We've got bad habits holding us back.

According to researcher and self-improvement specialist, James Clear, the reason is that your body is continually building habits. Oxford University researchers have found that compared to newborns, adult humans have over 40 percent fewer neurons. Clear says this is because your brain is actively pruning away connections between neurons that don't get used, and at the same time, reinforcing the connections you use regularly. It makes your brain work more efficiently, but it makes it much harder to change.

Because the habit is such a strong subconscious force, you can use it as a self-persuasion method by building new habits that help you.

Habit Stacking

The term "habit stacking" comes from S. J. Scott's 2014 book by the same name. In their work, Scott and Clear propose that you "piggyback" a valuable habit you want to create onto a habit you already have. For example, you need to do a better job of loading the dishes in the dishwasher regularly, instead of just leaving them in the sink. You have a habit of listening to your favorite podcast every day. If you change your podcast habit to listening in the kitchen when it's time to load the dishwasher, you'll soon create a habit of loading the dishwasher while listening to your podcast. The new, desirable behavior connects with the existing habit.

This works best with small tasks that can easily be combined to treat them as one habit. The power of habit stacking is to make excellent and easy habits interlocked so you always do one with the other. Eventually, the good habit becomes just as strong as the original habit because of neuron pathways' pruning to favor what we often do and eliminate what we don't often do.

Making a Well-Worn Path

When attempting to use self-persuasion to make any changes in your behavior, it's best to set up a path for yourself ahead of time so that you have little chance to go astray until you've established the new actions as a habit. Chip and Dan Heath, in their book, Switch, compare behavior to the relationship between an elephant, a rider, and their path. You can direct the rider (being our conscious mind) only so well when the mind is our own. The elephant, being our emotions and subconscious mind, will take some direction but in the end will go where it damn well pleases. But the elephant can be controlled ultimately by the path it is on. If the path is well-defined and challenging to stray from, even the most substantial elephant must follow along. To change a behavior, shape the path for your elephant so that the habit will form quickly.

Recognizing Self-Persuasion Tactics

We all like to believe and think that we are safe and immune from others' control and we are free to make our own decisions. With the advent of the Internet and social media, positive thinkers were calling this time the new Age of Information, where all information would be available to all people, all of the time. Never would people again be without the valuable facts they needed to make the best decisions about their lives. People would find peace and understanding as we all started to see more central ground as we had a better sense of shared experience worldwide. Each person would be able to make their voice heard.

How is this working out? Not so well. Some people think this is a most divided nation, especially along political lines. If you were to judge public discourse only by what you see online, you would expect to see rioting in the streets. When you talk to people face-to-face, though, you see that things are not nearly so black-and-white. What's going on?

Persuasion in Overdrive

Much of what you're seeing is persuasion in overdrive because of the Internet. As you've seen in the principles and techniques we've given you for persuasion, communication is the fundamental component of all kinds of persuasion. The always-on nature of communication today has just increased the communication channels we all have available to us tenfold.

But isn't that supposed to make us all smarter and more well-informed? Getting all of those facts at the tap of a screen should make it, so we never get fooled. How can so many people come to so many disparate decisions on what is right and wrong? As usual, the human mind is at fault.

Welcome to the Age of Selective Reality

Carnegie Mellon University researchers published a paper in the

Journal of Economic Literature. They found that people have developed what they call "information-avoidance strategies" that keep them only hearing what they want to hear.

Of course, we need to edit the stream of information. The Internet is like a fire hose of data, so we need to curate the information we receive. But according to research, people are adept at subconsciously paying attention to the communication that reinforces what they already believe and what reflects well on themselves, while selectively forgetting information they wish was not right. This bias serves as an excellent means of leading you to self-persuasion. Nobody told you to believe a certain way, but it was because you were given only information that led you to think a certain way. Your freedom of choice led you astray.

The Advent of Fake News

The media doesn't help. Once a fact-checked, attribution-required record of facts is now a re-tweeted, live posted, a be-first-not-right mob of professional social media echo chamber makers. Reporters are people, too. If they are putting their opinions out there, they will gravitate toward the information that makes them look good. They use the 6 Principles of Persuasion, either consciously or subconsciously, to keep getting you to click, like, and follow them. Facts are subjective, as they say.

Once, only advertising was allowed to behave in this overtly persuasive way. But now, all information is fair game. It is about news as entertainment, and the communicators need your attention to keep advertising revenue flowing. Welcome to the era of Fake News. Fake News refers to information passed off as fact when its prime purpose is to persuade you to do something.

This "news" may or may not have any truth behind it at all. As we have shown so far, persuasion techniques can be used for any purpose. The principles aren't dependent on facts; they rely only on human behavior, which is fairly predictable. To protect yourself from persuasion meant to manipulate you against your own best interest, you need to start casting a more discerning eye toward the messages you receive every day. To tell the difference between persuasion and fact, you can apply what you now know about persuasion techniques to sift through what you are being told.

Use Your Fact Barometer

Dr. Sander van der Linden, an Assistant Professor of Psychology at the University of Cambridge, offers the following questions as a barometer of whether you should allow something you hear to persuade you as fact.

First, watch for content that is politically themed. Increasing polarization helps keep you clicking, and giving you something to agree or disagree with immediately is one way to make you pick sides.

Then, social media content should be automatically suspect. Facts rarely go viral. If everybody is talking about it, take another look. What is the source of this information? Facts should attribute to a trusted source, not merely another website or blogger. Facts should be verified from more than one source and used in the proper context. And, if it sounds too ridiculous or over-the-top to be true, it probably is. We all know how "clickbait" works. Something crazy in your newsfeed begs you to click it to see what's going on. The more competition, the more outlandish the headline needs to be to get attention. Facts tend not to be that interesting.

Have You Been Informed, or Persuaded?

Recognizing the techniques of self-persuasion as they are applied to ourselves is when a simple "gut check" is not going to be a good indicator. When the information is geared to persuade rather than inform, you need to apply conscious effort and logic to find the truth. Analyze messages you receive against the principles' framework to see if new information you receive is something you can believe or if it requires a bit of independent fact-checking to get to the real facts.

Conclusion

Persuasion, manipulation, naked influence, and the art of reading people's mind are concepts that will aid you in getting the end result you want to see. They all have some basic differences, but the similarity is that they are all a form of human communication. As humans, we are easily changed by what we see and listen to each day.

The power of persuasion techniques is outstanding when executed flawlessly. One can't resist the opportunity to ace them if the person in question is functioning as a sales executive. The persuasion technique training isn't some simple training. The power of persuasion can likewise be obtained by another procedure called the natural training process. In this training, the learners are encouraged to peruse the customer's mind. Without a safety buffer, they will be effectively addressing the target with words they might want to hear so that in the end, they can influence him or her to purchase the item.

The power of persuasion is recognized in fruitful sales executives who have made it in to business magazines. Even normal people with instinct through words and appearance can exert persuasion They have effectively learned to utilize their skills to turn the choice of a customer to their benefit.

The power of persuasion is the mystery behind the sales individual's control over the unsuspecting customer. The minute you win the trust of your customer, the activity of persuasion is done, selling an item is a cakewalk.

Power of persuasion is a delicate skill to wield. It is imperative to strike up a discussion first. Of course, keep your aims imperceptible. When you see that you are controlling the progression of the discussion, you should affability incite the desired motivation to "take the bait".

The power of persuasion is behind any successful sales division of a corporate entity. The impact of the technique done right has created fortunes.